Natural Selection
of Political Forces

Natural Selection of Political Forces

by

Adolf A. Berle, Jr.

Professor of Law,
Columbia University

University Press of Kansas
Lawrence and London

PRINTED IN THE UNITED STATES OF AMERICA

Prefatory Note

The main substance of this book was originally delivered in April, 1948, as the second series of lectures given at Lawrence in honor of Judge Nelson Timothy Stephens, a founder of the University of Kansas Law School. I have, however, considerably modified and enlarged the text in the light of changing world conditions.

The Judge Stephens Lectureship of the School of Law is supported by an endowment left by his daughter, Miss Kate Stephens, an alumna of the University.

July 14, 1950   Adolf A. Berle, Jr.

Preface to Revised Edition

These essays were written exactly twenty years ago. Their intent was to test a fundamental thesis. Political science theretofore had been chiefly descriptive. Careful studies had been made of political developments. Clearly the course of historical development was being determined by currents of ideas, made effective through national organizations such as political parties and international organizations, regional or world-wide. Nationalist political forces struggle for and attain mastery of the government of States. In larger aspect, they effect tenuous groupings of States, since governments expressing similar idea-systems tend to work together.

In 1948, two such groupings were evident—the Communist States, then under the monolithic leadership of the Soviet Union, and liberal-democratic States, then polarizing around the leadership of the United States. Previously a competing political force—dictatorial Fascism—had brought about a grouping of European States (Nazi Germany, Fascist Italy, and a few smaller satellites). These had waged war both against the Communist and against the liberal-democratic countries. Their complete defeat in 1945 had, for the time at least, destroyed Fascism as a political force.

Attempt had been made, chiefly at the instance of President Franklin D. Roosevelt, to bridge the gap between these two forces. He hoped that through the Yalta agreements of 1945 the chief territorial disputes had been settled. He had arranged for the erection of a world organization—the United Nations—whose central mechanism might solve the detailed problems arising between the two groups as matters developed. He had himself examined the United Nations drafts arrived at through the Dumbarton Oaks discussions. Substantial agreement had been achieved on the methods and rules by which the United Nations would function. Though he died in April, 1945, the plan Roosevelt had stimulated and approved was adopted at San Francisco. The Charter of the United Nations was signed on June 26, 1945, and ratification duly followed.

Within this framework, it was believed competing political forces could operate but could adjust their differences without resort to force.

One element, however, had been underestimated. Few realized the depth of antagonism felt by the Soviet Union and the Communist-oriented political forces grouped around it against the liberal-democratic States, although most of them had been allies of the Soviet Union during World War II. Under the leadership of the late Joseph Stalin, who united the Communist idea-system to historic imperialist Russian nationalism, the Soviet Union proposed to take as much territory and dominate as many other States as it could. His method was to use or set up political parties in other states responsive to Soviet-Communist authority, and to assist these overtly or covertly by Soviet arms or diplomacy, or both. It was easy to impose Communist political structures and idea-systems on all of the States occupied, as the war ended, by Soviet troops; this is how the Iron Curtain countries of Central Europe and the East German Zone of occupation came to have (as they still do) Communist governments.

As these essays were being presented, the Stalinist government was subsidizing and assisting political and para-military action designed to take over the governments of most other Western European States. It was active in China and its neighboring States, notably Korea and Viet Nam.

Shortly after the lectures in this volume were delivered, Soviet political and military pressure forced resignation of the liberal-democratic government of Czechoslovakia, replacing it with a Moscow-dominated regime. By virtue of military occupation, Moscow had erected North Korea into a Communist State. The Soviet Union was pushing in all directions, endeavoring to bring as much territory as lay within reach under the Communist idea-system and Communist political organization and—not incidentally —under direct control of the Soviet Union. Winston Churchill christened the vast game "the Cold War." Such was the competition between political forces in 1948.

While these essays were in leisurely process of publication, the situation took a violent turn. On June 25, 1950, under Soviet sponsorship, some 60,000 Russian-supplied North Korean troops crossed the occupation line (the 38th Parallel) dividing the Soviet from the American Zone of occupation. Their plan was to seize South Korea, then firmly in the hands of an independent Korean government headed by Mr. Syngman Rhee. Competition between the two principal political forces in the world thus reached the stage of open war. At instance of the United

States, the United Nations and its Security Council promptly dealt with the situation, authorizing organization of an United Nations force and the defense of South Korea. Of this force, the United States supplied most of the men, most of the arms, and the command. In right of the United Nations, the Korean war was waged as a "peace-keeping" operation.

The nations of most of the world now were called on to choose between the two competing forces—Stalinist Communism (the schisms dividing the Communist group were not then acute) and the so-called "free"—that is, liberal-democratic—world. This is why I included "Epilogue, 1950: The Valley of Decision" as final comment. In this new edition, I have let it stand as written—choice between competing political forces was then presented to almost all the nation-States on earth.

The Korean war, as we know, resulted in a successful defense of South Korea—at least for the time being. It did not resolve the problem of the competing world-wide political forces. That competition has both continued and changed character during the two decades since these essays appeared. Communism as a political force has divided into two main stems—one an expression of Russian nationalism, another an expression of a turbulent Chinese nationalism; yet everywhere (for example, in Czechoslovakia, Rumania, and Yugoslavia, and even in Cuba) nationalism seems to assert itself. On the "free world" side, the same tendency appears: France overtly embraced nationalism as guiding policy of the DeGaulle government, almost wrecking the unity of Western Europe.

Hence, in this new edition a second epilogue suggesting the selections of political forces possible at present. Once more competition has flamed into warfare in Viet Nam and elsewhere, though the political forces in conflict have changed their nature. It is possible that a climactic confrontation—perhaps in the Mediterranean Sea—may emerge in the not too distant future.

As I hope to make clear, political forces competing for support have substantially changed in the two decades elapsing between the first and this revised edition. The principle of selection has not. The "Epilogue, 1968" reflects the different implications contained in selecting among political forces active now rather than those which prevailed in 1950.

July, 1968   ADOLF A. BERLE

Contents

Prologue, 1948:
Philosophy and Fear

This phenomenon has been steadily repeated throughout world history. In modern times alone, there was major re-examination and re-statement of political values at the time of the Reformation; again at the time of the French Revolution with its ensuing Napoleonic struggles; again, during the 19th-century contest between the conception of a world based on science and the conception of a world deriving its knowledge also through revelation and religion. This latest contest, indeed, may well be responsible for the rise of materialist totalitarianism. That rise generated one climax in the Second World War, and clearly the end is not yet.

With varying effect, in each period, men have stated their faith, backing it with such proof and verification as the scientific and scholarly method of the time permitted.

In this 20th century, certain methods are no longer generally accepted, and the result has narrowed considerably the means by which any declaration of values can be supported. During most of world history, divine revelation was considered authoritative in great areas. Although today masses of humanity still accept revelation as authority, a majority of the literate world appears to insist on scientific verification,—though the case against revelation is far from being as closed as some suppose.

But if verification is limited by apparent loss of certain older avenues to knowledge, its possibilities have been augmented by development of others. The authority of scientific demonstration is accepted—perhaps indeed over-accepted — to a point where, within their own field, scientists have an authority not unlike that of the medieval

4

church. Other techniques of scholarship and discipline have evolved methods of establishing truth in greater or lesser degree. The 20th century is at least as well equipped to state conclusions of enduring truth as were groups of 19th-century scientists, each of whom made a permanent contribution towards the organization of human life.

The life of the world of today is at once highly organized, and, at the same time, in danger of dissolution. Mechanical, political, and ideological structures are vaster and more nearly world-wide than at any time in recorded history. Yet the individual's confidence in these structures is, apparently, less firm than at any period in modern times. True, there is a general faith in the data of mechanical and physical scientific development. But these are neutral, in the sense that they supply no guide either for individual or for collective life. Pure science can provide mathematical equations, equally useful in dissolving the atom as a prelude to constructing a bomb, or in charting the distant stars. Physical science can create gunpowder, which is equally useful for Chinese celebrations or for killing. Bacteriology can create serums equally capable of saving life or of loosing disease to devastate an enemy.

Values, permanent, or at least enduring, as a basis for the construction of the life of an individual, family, nation, an empire, or world order, do not, on the other hand, rest on any universally accepted base. The word of a scientist in his neutral field is taken at face value. The word of a philosopher, priest, politician, or economist, is not.

One result has been that at this, the mid-point in the 20th century, an outstanding fact is the phenomenon of

5

universal fear—sometimes expressed and acted upon, sometimes dull and concealed, but omnipresent, save, perhaps in the case of the few remaining savage tribes living in their native wildernesses.

All of us have seen this phenomenon at every level of life.

A nascent community of nations fears (and slumbers at the brink of) its dissolution and a new world war, which could surpass in intensity of horror everything which has gone before.

Nations fear, and some are experiencing, the breakup of their internal structure, and have the greater fear that the disaster of collapse may be followed by the still greater disaster of inability to reconstruct. Some, indeed, driven by that fear, have already sought escape by endeavoring to forbid thought, and by establishing ruthless, totalitarian-police states. Of these, three—Nazi Germany, Fascist Italy, and Imperial Japan—have already discovered that this is no road to escape, but rather a blind plunge into catastrophe.

Within nations, communities fear the dissolution of kindly and friendly and productive relationships, and the growth of hatred and conflict between group and group—racial, economic or social. As this tendency increases, smaller groups tend to be torn apart. Even families fear the breaking of the most intimate relationships of life; indeed, sociologically the weakening of the family structure is a conspicuous 20th-century phenomenon whether at Moscow, London, Los Angeles, or Nanking.

Individual men and women carry a fear which few of

them understand. Cultured men, struggling to become citizens of the world, and to make a world which permits such citizens, of course, can comprehend their tremendous loss as they find it increasingly difficult not only to realize their great and generous dreams, but even to stand on common ground within their own countries with their own occupational associates, their own group of friends, their own families. Less literate minds understand quite perfectly the fear of want and of international or civil war, or more simply the dread that they, or their children, will die horribly on the periphery of the explosion radius of an atom bomb. Whether literate or instinctive, both vaguely know that these are only manifestations of underlying and deeper cause. The source-fear is more profound.

Quite simply stated, the pervading and paralyzing shadow is fear that neither man nor life has value at all. Even worse: that man in general and men as individuals never did have meaning or value and never can have; that hopes, faiths, creeds, religions, philosophies setting out values or truths, were folk-tales told to comfort or delude children or fools.

Compared to the results of this fear, an atom bomb is trivial. For when an individual loses belief in any value or any meaning whatever, he is condemned to a fate beyond the dreams of Dante. He must and he can think only of himself—and even that is no great matter. He must live as an animal does, fighting a rear-guard action with time against his ultimate and unimportant death. His social relations become animal: He satisfies his immediate desires as he can, hunts his prey, runs with a pack if and when it is possible and as long as it serves him or the pack; he betrays or is torn to pieces by the pack as convenience serves either—and that, too, does not matter. A babble of voices calls him here or there—inviting him to join this pack, to surrender that freedom, to forget or amputate part or all of his consciousness; promising him in return anything from a full dinner pail to a share in some one else's idea of the "historical process." But these voices belong only to other animals like himself—who are also nothing, fighting their own losing struggle with consciousness, seeking to swallow him as a part of their equally meaningless individual and pitiful defense against chaos.

The fear is a fear of the anarchy of nihilism, from which there is no refuge; the fear of being nothing, in a world which is itself nothing.

We should be happy if this were an imaginary sketch. Yet we have all seen it. We have seen statesmen and diplomats putting deceptively bold faces on the minor and often irrelevant theatricals of negotiations and international conferences. We have seen it in doctor's offices where patients come to be cured of something—but the something over-passes physiology or chemistry. We have seen it when commissar or gauleiter, slavishly following his handbook of tactics and his untouchable textbook of principles, in sheer terror turns on some unimportant official who has questioned or revolted. (He, perhaps better than anyone else, knows that the same tactics will eventually destroy him and his untouchable profession of faith as it has already destroyed and weakened his fellows.)

This may well have been the state of mind of much of

the world at the time of great historical changes. Perhaps the pagan world felt like this when the whisper came that Pan might die, and that the goddess Domiduca could no longer help a traveler safely home. So, for that matter, a Persian may have felt when Alexander demonstrated that the laws of the Medes and the Persians could change. It may not have been an accident that in times like those the world turned to philosophers, religious or secular.

In recent decades, many of the so-called "best minds" have contributed little to the philosophic front, save prophecies of disaster. One of the greatest of American philosopher-historians, Henry Adams, addressed the American Historical Association in 1909 and forecast with uncanny accuracy the material development of the world out of the age of steam and electricity into the age of radioactivity and atomic energy, laying down for that change a time schedule which is a masterpiece of prophetic insight. But he could only compute that the world would struggle hopelessly with this rising scale of uncontrollable force, arriving at chaos about the year 1953. The outstanding German philosopher of history, Oswald Spengler, christened his famous book "The Decline of the West," closing on the cheerful note that the western world, if indeed not all the world, was beyond salvation. The physical scientists have powerfully forecast the horrors in store for the world as it uses the amoral forces they have unlocked. Many of them have sought solace in an endeavor to erect a structure of society capable of controlling these forces. Unhappily, never having analyzed social structures with the same care with which they have analyzed an atom, they can only clamor for more political machinery, at the precise moment when there is growing lack of confidence in any kind of political machinery at all. Nihilism almost approaches the status of doctrine in the case of existentialist philosophy which proclaims that there is no answer.

The history of these phenomena, however, is fairly traceable. For present purposes, the story can be picked up in the latter part of the 19th century, at which time a considerable part of the western intellectual world became concerned with the so-called "warfare between science and religion." Moral and personal values at that time had been considered to be the province of divines, claiming authority from revelation, though they buttressed their conclusions by occasional mobilization of observed phenomena from the physical world. The scientists, notably Darwin and Huxley, on pure observations of physical data, reached conclusions as to the development of man and the physical world which were thought to be inconsistent with these revelations. The Book of Genesis ceased thus to be a statement coming from God, and was reduced to a rather inaccurate collection of legends; and, openly or tacitly, most of the thinking world considered that the basis of all religion was shattered.

It is scarcely an accident that an a priori materialist like Karl Marx was able to gain acceptance of his purely materialist theory of social structure just when a breach in theism had been opened by the Victorian scientists. It is certainly no accident that Germany, which went farther and faster down the purely scientific road than any other country, most completely lost connection with any previous set of values, and most readily swallowed a crude collection of gibberish eventually offered by Hitler and his court-philosopher, Rosenberg, as a substitute in 1934. All statements of value or truths or meaning were placed on trial. It is a short step from that to the suggestion—and hence the fear —that there is no such thing as a value or a meaning or a truth anywhere. Only as brute force compels conformity to a certain set of premises for a limited period of time is there rational basis for anything; so Hitler set up a civilization on that premise.

The United States, which does not number among its more recent vices undue attention to abstract thinking, watched this process with only limited interest and concern. Americans were, of course, mistaken in that. Europeans took Nazism seriously because they knew some things Americans did not. They knew that a philosophical force is gossamer, spun of incomprehensible words; but they also knew that it can produce social results capable of knocking civilization to pieces. Europe had seen the Roman Empire organize Paganism on a philosophy of law; had seen obscure Christian theorists take over the Roman Empire; had seen the Reformation shatter the nearly achieved dream of a universal empire and tear countries to shreds; had seen philosophers bring about the rise of the French Revolution, its conversion into the Napoleonic Empire; and remembered the wreck of that structure. Europeans rightly refuse to consider philosophical theories as purely academic.

In the United States, the country as a whole learned that Shinto, Fascism, or Marxian materialism could mean also bullets and bombs only on the bitter Sunday of Pearl Harbor.

The historical truth is that society (national or international), communities (regional or local), individual relationships or families, and indeed the structure of an individual life, are possible only on a basis of philosophical values which attain individual expression. If it is bad to be a man without a country, it is worse to be a man without a premise. Indeed, if men have no premises, there can be no country or, for that matter, any other lasting social manifestation.

Yet values must be more than premises. The scientist may state that no set of values can be more than assumptions; that they constitute only a working hypothesis. Therefore, he continues, the hypothesis is always subject to attack; the structure is never firmly founded. The best you can do, he argues, is to have a good hypothesis and stay with it as long as you can. The older scientific doctrine would add "on that basis, one hypothesis is as good as another," but your philosopher would still attack the problem. Conceding that truth cannot be wholly arrived at either by revelation or reason, he would say that it is possible to make progress towards truth, however slow that progress is; and it is the task of men in general and all philosophers in particular to endeavor to increase the approximation of truth no matter how difficult the task. And here the scientist is forced to agree: for all his science is based on certain continuing observable rules or phenomena which he knows to be constant and therefore true; and he has results to prove it. If this is a pitifully small segment of truth as a permanent value, it still is enough to prevent the scientist from questioning the existence of any truth at all. Perhaps this conviction has saved scientists more than any other group from the prevailing fear.

In point of fact, exactly this discussion under historical circumstances not entirely dissimilar from the present was carried on by Aristotle at a research foundation in Macedonia while his former pupil, Alexander, was at once breaking and rebuilding two of the greatest empires of which history has knowledge. Even today, the entire world is still working within the limits of conceptions he then laid out; and the values he achieved, though they may not necessarily be eternal, have certainly proved enduring.

But the scientist, overthrowing revelation in the late 19th century, was merely beginning. In the following half-century he pushed through barrier after barrier previously supposed to be impassable. His cheerful assumption of materialism based on the end of transcendental truth began to shift and twist when he broke through some of the outer riddles of matter itself; reduced molecules to atoms, and smashed atoms to bits of abstract force, themselves held together by an unexplained abstraction. Actually, in the last decade, the scientist has been driven towards the hypothesis of a universal principle which is not material but abstract, and, literally, not of this world.

Now in various unconnected lines of scientific observation in fields heretofore considered unrelated, the lines are beginning to converge. This convergence tends, I think, to support the thesis of a central guiding conception, from which permanent values can be deduced and verified. Instead of Mr. Henry Adams' chaos, we may be on the threshold of rediscovering some principles of universal order.

"Natural Selection of Political Forces"

I

"Natural Selection of Political Forces"

§1

THESE ESSAYS are designed to examine a hypothesis in political science. The hypothesis here offered as the conclusion from the field of examination may be stated at the outset:

I. The law of political force—of any kind or order or magnitude—is governed in its creation and continuance by natural laws which appear to be invariable and constant.

II. There exists a law of selection of political forces somewhat analogous to the law of selection of species in the world of biology.

III. Selection favors political forces

(1) which tend to approach universality within their field of application; and

(2) which give to individuals a sense of harmony with the universal pattern.

Selection discards political forces

(1) which are based on limitative conceptions such as exclusion, aggrandizement, hatred, and the like; and

(2) which tend to concentrate power without modifying that power by imposing, in some form, corresponding responsibility.

The hypothesis involves the conception that the selection is not, ultimately, a matter of choice, but results from a law of social survival.

Like any law, human or natural, it can be defied, broken and, for a period of time, ignored. But in the end, the defiance, or opposition, causes the defeat or disintegration of the political force attempting such opposition, and its eventual disappearance. Such defeat or disintegration is a question of time; which may be longer or shorter depending on the aggregate of choice of the individuals within the political field in question. A political force, though doomed to disappearance, may be successful for a period of years or perhaps even for a period of centuries; but it nevertheless carries within itself its inescapable sentence of ultimate extinction.

Great assurance is required to present any principle as a "law" in the field of social science. Still greater assurance is needed to present as sweeping a hypothesis as this. Yet it is believed that the evidence we have fairly justifies the hypothesis. Nor need there be apology for the presentation. Certainly the condition of the political world at present requires boldness of scientific approach. Rather, explanation is called for from students of political science who have not yet attempted a synthesis, and have therefore left men as political animals to struggle in a world which appears to be anarchic.

The late Professor Cassirer of Yale closed his book, *The Myth of the State*—and with it his life's work—by writing a chapter which should be compulsory reading in every university course on government. He pointed out that social science, and particularly the science of politics,

is still a dream; that the attempts made thus far to give it
rational basis bear about the same relationship to the
science which one day will exist which medieval astrology
bears to modern astronomy. Auguste Comte attempted
such a hypothesis, trying to find an anology between social
science and natural science somewhat like that contem-
plated in these essays, though from an entirely different
standpoint; and, of course, Comte explored the subject before Darwin had laid the basis for rational explanation of
the biological world. Carlyle in his time had attempted to
build a synthesis of politics around the periodically appearing hero; *Heroes and Hero-Worship* was his great ef-
fort to make orderly arrangement of the apparently chaotic
forces whose records fill our history books, and whose results are filling the modern world with apparent confu-
sion. In our own lives, two philosophers have essayed the
same task, one, Oswald Spengler, pessimist, terrible and
severe; the other, Arnold Toynbee, optimist, humanist,
and kindly. Both are essentially mystic. Spengler in *The
Decline of the West* claimed to attempt for the first time
the venture of "predetermining" history; but history to
him was "predetermined" by an impersonal supra-natural
force called "destiny"—and Spengler's destiny predetermined us to complete disaster within a relatively short
space of historical time. It remained only for Spengler, as
interpreter, to prophesy the manner and extent of the
Apocalypse. Toynbee, likewise considering history predetermined by a doctrine of positive forces, found their
source in an equally supra-natural assumption of the good
—to him embodied in the Christian concept with its law

of love, around which the forces of history revolve, and towards which their eventual result must inevitably be drawn.

Both theses are essentially poetic. They are no less interesting on that account; speculations of poets are always worthy of respect. But neither carries rational conviction. Emotionally, a pessimist is predisposed to Spengler and ultimate catastrophe; while the optimist is predisposed to Toynbee and eventual triumph of kindlier forces. There is no premise by which the underlying assumption of either can be tested; no body of evidence which can be gathered, classified, and weighed; no demonstration, no method of demonstration.

One can understand why even a purely poetic attempt to make political forces intelligible excites human imagination. It is only necessary to contrast their reasoning with that of a historian-philosopher, Henry Adams, who attempted a hypothesis a generation ago. As president of the American Historical Association in 1909, he made an address to that august body which has come down to us under the title, *The Rule of Phase as Applied to History*. He traced changes in civilization to the change in man's ability to release natural force through its respective phases, solids, vapor, electronics, with eventual reduction to pure mathematics. As man became able to change matter from a solid or a liquid state into vapor—for instance, by using steam—civilization took on a new form, and its pace was vastly accelerated. When in time men learned to convert the energy thus developed into electricity, an "electronic age" occurred. This exhausted the positive phases of

20

matter. Accordingly, he believed the next stage must be reference to pure mathematics—the kind of mathematical speculation by which Einstein set the world on the path to atomic fission. Still greater acceleration of human force must result, thought Adams, and he accordingly prophesied (in 1909) the rapid growth of mechanical civilization through the decade of 1920, forecasting the mathematical discoveries which actually occurred about that time; and the subsequent liberation of the use of mathematics to break down even atomic structure. He arrived at the cheerful result that the world would find itself in complete chaos about 1953! It must be added that his prophecies of scientific development thus far have worked out with singular accuracy; the graph in his now famous essay is worth reproducing for the guidance of any politician. Naturally, healthy human minds shrink from accepting a sentence of death by chaos to be executed inside of four or five years; and by contrast with Henry Adams, a poet excites strong and favorable emotional bias.

Yet the problem remains. Men do not accept the inevitability of anarchy and chaos because, fundamentally, there is no more rational basis for assuming chaos, either in the universe or in politics, than to assume an ordered evolution. If anything, the idea of anarchy or chaos has less rational basis in a universe in which, sublimely disregarding the tiny though dangerous ideas with which men play, a solar system still holds together, which in turn is part of an infinite cosmos maintained in balance by apparently immutable laws.

Perhaps there is a narrower field within which we can

work, and by observing phenomena, find the guide to our answer. History is chiefly the record of endless human experiments in organization. These experiments have had more or less observable results. While we are far from having data as precise as that with which the natural scientists work, we cannot pretend that there is no body of evidence capable of being classified and interpreted. Whenever this condition exists, scholars are bound to attempt the task; to accumulate facts, to construct a hypothesis, and to expose that hypothesis for further examination.

This is a compulsion laid upon all of us who work in the social sciences. In little, or in great, we are testing the premises from which a philosophy of history will one day be born; and with it a science of politics, no less useful than the science which has given us our material civilization. A tiny fragment of that search forms the subject of these essays.

§2

A political force consists of a centrally attractive idea surrounded by an organizational apparatus. This combination—a nuclear idea with a surrounding apparatus—appears to be constant, whether the political force is as huge as a revolution, or as tiny as a local movement. Political forces enter into practically every compartment of recorded and unrecorded history. "Political" is here used in the Aristotelian sense—"politics" being the organization of power in any form.

Constant in all political force is the nucleus of ideas and conceptions here called a "centrally attractive idea." The writer has yet to find any visible organization of power in any category of human life, on any plane, which did not depend from such a nucleus. At one time it was thought that the primitive or savage was released from this; Rousseau, and later Chateaubriand, endeavored to create the idea of the "noble savage" with a blank and unclouded mind, moved by pure and "natural" impulse. Alas for this thought that there might be a child of nature happily unspoiled by politics! Anthropology has now taught us that the primitive is the least free man on earth. From cradle to grave, he, his family relationships, his method of life, and his manner of death, are determined by a set of myths and magic within which are comprised nuclear ideas that place him in firm relation to the human and natural world. More complicated forms of society, familiar to us, appear less bound because the nuclear ideas are less rigid or because there is possibility of choice between political forces; but, whether we are dealing with an organization like, let us say, the University of Kansas or the Catholic Church, the Elks Club or the Soviet Union, the company union or the Western European Defense Federation, we find that each is giving effect, though with varying objective, to a central conception. Probably no two individuals could maintain a continuous relationship with each other without such a nucleus.

If this be true, our first definition of political force must be in terms of its ideological content. What are the ideas on which the grouping was constructed? Are they valid for its continuance? For the purpose of this discussion, political forces are classifiable primarily in terms of ideas.

Almost immediately we discover that any unit of political force has a second aspect—a combination of methods, persuasion, incentives, and pressures by which individuals are held in organization or relationship to achieve the ends sought by the political force. It is necessary to coin a word for this second aspect. I adopt a word chiefly because a great part of the world uses it: the word "apparatus." Apparatus now includes the entire range of method, from persuasion and emotion to force, persecution, and compulsion, by which groups are held together. In combination, the nucleus and the apparatus set up a political force. As we shall see, the political force may, and perhaps usually does, acquire through its apparatus, ends and objectives not comprehended in, and possibly incompatible with, the ideological nucleus. This highly important process will call for later examination. It is enough here to note the point that political force, like the physical atom, is composite, and may be broken down.

Political forces historically have reached their most powerful development in huge swings of social and governmental organization which we call "revolution." Because political forces are more easily observable and their effects more fully recorded in revolution than in other times, the historical phenomena here examined largely have to do with revolutions. This has, today, the transient (but human) value of making our study not merely observation of the academic past, but analysis of the throbbing and dangerous present. We shall find ourselves considering not merely the record of previous political forces, but the crashing interplay of forces which already have powerfully affected—and will further powerfully affect—the lives of all of us. It happens that we live in a revolutionary time, in which political forces have become so concentrated that at present they dominate, for better or for worse, the overwhelming majority of all human life on this planet.

§3

A useful and illustrative prelude to examination of the present may nevertheless be found in a revolution of the distant past. We here take one as illustration of the method of our research. Analysis of it will, perhaps, even give some guide to the drama to which we are daily treated in our morning newspapers.

The year was 1215; the place was England. Political forces were as active then as they are in Asia or Central Europe now. Probably to the contemporaneous observer they looked as blind and confusing as does a revolution in Yugoslavia or Middle Asia today. A weak king, John, was endeavoring to consolidate his political power. His centrally attractive idea, nuclear to his political force, was his God-given throne, and the popular belief that the king was God's anointed military and civil dictator. Accepted ideology thus elevated him into an almost magic myth—perhaps actually magic, for the king was supposed to have power to work certain minor miracles such as curing scrofula. For apparatus, he had the pomp and ceremony which was part of his task; and a certain control over the peace of the realm which was slowly hardening into law—the law being the "King's justice," and besides, he controlled a moderate-sized army. On the economic side, he held certain powers of dispensing and withholding favors, with the right if not the duty to apply force to carry out his will.

This king had the temerity to endeavor to extend his royal prerogative into fields which many of his great nobles considered reserved for them, and to handle his dispensing of patronage so as to excite both their jealousy and their fear. His barons banded together to assert demands upon the Crown, or if need be oppose its wearer. They formed, in our terminology, an opposing "political force." This grouping seems to have been brought about chiefly by the common interest of a powerful class in favor of maintaining its own position, wealth, and strength. What ideas other than these originally brought them together is a matter of obscure history; but it does appear that they had some common body of thought, stated in not wholly selfish terms, which furnished a common denominator.

The king's party and the nobles' party (inspired, let us assume like any Marxian, primarily by selfishness) came into conflict. The nobles' party proved stronger. After some military maneuvering, the king found himself substantially at the mercy of this small, strong, privileged, and heavily armed class. The two sides met at Runnymede to determine a course of action. The result of that meeting was the document we know today as Magna Carta, forerunner of the entire conception of civil liberties, of the American Bill of Rights, cornerstone of Anglo-Saxon justice throughout the great part of the world.

In actual fact, Magna Carta constituted a set of limitations on the field of royal power, and a series of guarantees of barons' privileges. It is a fair inference that the barons who exacted the charter were mainly interested in extorting a pledge that the feudal estates given their ancestors by William the Norman and his descendants, should not be taken from them by the king; and that their property and seignorial rights should be otherwise protected. That was probably the content, for them, of the "liberties and laws of England," to which they appealed. The clear personal motivation was desire for, and the effect was to ensure them, secure possession of the properties and special privileges of their powerful and arrogant class. Their political force was held together by a dialectic of self-interest and military organization.

A modern observer—let us say a political writer for the *Kansas City Star*—leaping backwards seven and a half centuries, would draw little inspiration from it. He would note the centrally attractive idea they propounded: the appeal to law and ancient liberties. He would be interested in the political device used: insistence that the defeated king bind the Crown forever to observe the legal customs and laws set up by his predecessors, who had, by fiat, established the law of England. He would be painfully aware that hardly a baron at Runnymede had the faintest interest in the fate of the common man, or in the liberties or well-being of the people of England. If any individual had such a concern, certainly the baronial party as a whole did not. The formula they used was plainly a handy and useful tool to entrench them in the privileges they held and desired to expand. Our reporter might even do a little muckraking about Magna Carta. An uninspiring, selfish performance all around. That would probably be his verdict.

Yet history has taken that political force apart, has sorted out its respective elements, has regrouped them, and has drawn out of this somewhat sordid conflict a constant nucleus of ideas which has repeatedly motivated political forces of steadily growing strength unto this very day. For, in drawing their charter, the baronial party undertook to express a centrally attractive idea: an ideology cast in terms of justice under law, whose benefits and reciprocal duties rested on all alike. Barons could appeal to this principle to safeguard their huge estates; but then, so also could any freeman with a farm. It mattered little, as men's minds developed, that the clauses protecting a freeman or a villein were probably inserted in 1215 so that the freeman or the villein would continue to cultivate the farm of the great lord from whom he held it. The statement of the doctrine was so cast that it *did* say something to substantially everyone. When later groups of barons wished new protection, as they did, and asked further confirmation of the Runnymede charter, their political efforts necessarily carried along with them the rights of others which were assimilated to their own.

It is unnecessary here to trace further the law and the long, familiar history of Magna Carta. Baronial parties came and went. Kings sought to recoup their unlimited power, momentarily succeeded, were faced by a political force once more grouped around the old idea, which once more collected a new apparatus; kings were again defeated and almost vanished. The conception of liberty under law and under a constitutionally limited government was able to call apparatus into being and become a political force over and over again. It does today, long after the class of feudal barons who first appealed to it have passed into history.

For us, the fascinating fact is that out of the congeries of political forces existing together in the thirteenth century, this one survived while others were defeated, or fell into atrophy and eventually died. Analytically it is clear that there were present in the little island in the Thames a variety of potential political forces: the royal absolutism, for one; the baronial oligarchy, for another; possibly some idealist desire to improve the lot of England (the bishops, clerks, scriveners, and canon lawyers in the various camps may conceivably have had some such notion). Certainly the apparatus on both sides was quite free of major preoccupation with questions of social progress or ideal political development. King John's chiefly revolved around loyalty to king inspired by hope of gain or fear of punishment. The opposition apparatus reflected loyalty to a group of barons inspired by substantially similar motives. Uniting their apparatus with the central conception of the law and liberty of England, the barons consolidated a political as well as a military force. The revolution began by winnowing out and discarding complete autocracy as a dominant political force—a clear historical case of selection between rival political forces.

Later, when the baronial party no longer clung to the ideology of constitutional civil rights and substantially seized the kingdom, another historic selection took place.

The barons at length fell with the Earl of Warwick, at the end of the civil war known as the War of the Roses. The Crown had now appropriated the ideology of constitutional civil rights and it emerged triumphant. Still later, when it was conceived that the Tudors and their Stuart successors had deserted the ideological conception, new groups formed an apparatus based on this ideology, became a political force, and further limited the power of the Crown. Indeed the United States was born of one of the late phases of this continued selection: the Crown was considered to have deserted and violated the conception of liberty under the laws of England as applied to the American colonies. Restating the doctrine, now augmented by the ideas of the French political philosopher, Rousseau, Jefferson restated the thesis in the Declaration of Independence; Washington, Adams, Franklin, Randolph, and others created an apparatus; and, in a new phase, a political force took form which brought into existence the American republic.

Nor is the power of the central conception spent today. The precise and appealing quality of the doctrine of Runnymede was its affirmation of certain rights to all— the fact that it was of universal application within its country. Only three years ago a Committee on Civil Rights was named by the President of the United States with instruction to inquire into and determine whether and in what respect current law enforcement measures of federal, state, and local governments may be strengthened and improved to safeguard the civil rights of the people. The report of that Committee "To Secure These Rights" is already a classic, and has already been a major political issue. In 1948, as an answer to a message of the President requesting legislation implementing the report, seven governors of Southern states replied by organizing the apparatus of a counter-political force, whose nucleus was the conception of "white supremacy" and local autonomy in civil rights matters. Once more the issue is joined; a new contest impends which will eventually result in selection of one or other force. The long story is never done.

For so long as men continue to exist as social animals, their political processes not only do but must select from among political forces available. As will appear if they make a wrong selection, the chosen political force, soon or late, breaks up and disappears. In politics, as in nature, there is freedom to choose. In politics, as in nature, bad selection weakens the ability to survive.

§4

It is one thing to take a single and dramatic illustration of a continuing political force as a text, but quite another to use that illustration as a basis for sweeping generalization. We should have no right to use the survival of a political force grouped around the conception of constitutional liberty as evidence of selection, unless selection appeared from examination of other historical data.

Therefore, still using revolutions as our chief laboratory material, we must attempt to examine a number of these with a view to discovering whether there is similar history of the survival of some political forces; similar record of the discarding of others. In doing so, it will save time if we examine the phenomena of revolutions in general.

We should expect to find, and it is the fact, that great revolutions do have certain qualities in common. In the last century, Professor Lyford Paterson Edwards described this fact in a fascinating volume, *The Natural History of Revolutions* (published in 1878), which still remains a classic in its field. Later, Dr. Crane Brinton studied the phenomena from a different angle. Today, we could further document Edwards' main conclusions. The unhappily great experience in revolutions which we have had since 1878 would hardly challenge his central thesis. We shall, indeed, add one conclusion which he did not draw; but it flows from and does not conflict with Edwards' own observations.

A revolution invariably affirms certain values in the field of morals. These form indeed the ideological nucleus at the center of the revolutionary political force. The strength of the revolution is derived in principal measure from the yearning for, or at least the acquiescence of men in, these values. But revolutions invariably include as a part of their method or apparatus military or paramilitary force, carried if need be to the point of civil conflict. At Runnymede, mobilization of force was enough. More often, great revolution means also civil war.

At this point the ideological nucleus is clothed in a political apparatus which imposes, rigidly and often brutally, the logic of its ideology. As Professor Edwards put it, revolution is the exact reverse of anarchy. It is coalescence of force to impose the idea. As it reaches its climax the revolution is not absence of law, it *is* law—of a sort. Should it degenerate into anarchy the revolution is lost: another nucleus will gather around it an apparatus and will establish itself as the stronger political force in the situation. Not infrequently, when this occurs, it is merely a regrouping of the political force which the revolution was intended to destroy; a regrouping so usual that it has acquired the historical name "counterrevolution." A successful revolution, led by practical men, understands this perfectly; accordingly, its first concern is to hold its own forces together in iron discipline, and its second is to prevent any grouping, anywhere, around any nucleus of ideas other than its own. To do otherwise is to imperil the success of the revolution, and, incidentally, the lives of the revolutionists.

Revolution, consequently, usually results in the creation of a military or quasi-military dictatorship. If the dictatorship is not created out of the revolution itself, it supervenes at the moment the revolution shows signs of weakening into anarchy. In modern times, there is almost unbroken history to support this observation. Certainly it proved true in the Russian Revolution of 1917. Then, a democratic revolution brought about by the desire for peace, land, opportunity, and democracy, weakly permitted a more violent ideology, Leninist-Marxism, to group around it the full vigor of a totalitarian apparatus. The strain of continued war threatened the Kerenski government with disintegration; and the Leninist dictatorship took over without difficulty. This was also the history of the French Revolution: a political force based on the concept of constitutional liberty weakened by attack from without, suffered counter-revolution from within. The Constitutional Assembly increasingly ceded power to Marat, Danton, Robespierre, then to the Directoire. Finally a dynamic young artillery general named Napoleon, appropriating the conceptions of the revolution and using artillery and his army as apparatus, tossed the whole edifice overboard, and made himself first dictator-emperor in fact, then emperor in name as well.

No less was this true of the great revolutions which attended the Reformation and the rise of Protestantism in Europe. Perhaps the prototype of the modern totalitarian revolution was that of Oliver Cromwell. Beginning in the name of religious liberty, with a central conception so grand that it commanded the support of the poet Milton, the Civil War maintained by the Long Parliament engendered an oligarchy which in turn gave rise to the autocracy of a single man. Cromwell, after enjoying the fact of dictatorial power for some years, took a title likewise, proclaiming himself Lord Protector, with absolute power, thinly disguised by a puppet assembly. One can go through the catalog of true revolutions (as distinguished from mere changes in government without substantial change in the ideological system), finding scarcely an exception.

Even our own American Revolution only barely escaped this fate. Beginning with the conception of constitutional liberty and the apparatus of democratic government, a cabal of officers feared the weakness of the ensuing government and sought to crown Washington king. He rejected this out of hand; it is one of his many proofs of

34

great statesmanship. After he left office, in the time of John Adams, somewhat similar plots reappeared; both Alexander Hamilton and Aaron Burr appear to have toyed with the idea of setting up a military or property-holding oligarchy; Jefferson, clinging to the Revolution, was elected in 1800 only by a hair's breadth.

Revolution is a political force which tends to realize its central idea by the apparatus of dictatorship and arms. As we shall see, the apparatus and the idea at once become opposed to each other.

§5

At this point note must be made of a phenomenon which appears to be constant in the composition of political forces. A political force is, as we have seen, a centrally attractive idea or conception, surrounded, or organized, by an apparatus. But it appears that there is an antithesis between the apparatus and the central conception.

Put more dramatically, the apparatus, whether it be army, hierarchy, political bureaucracy, or popular organization, in some measure is at war with the central idea. Further, the more powerful and highly organized the apparatus, the greater the antithesis between it and the central conception.

One may speculate on the reason for this. It approximates the reciprocal repulsions and attractions between the positive and negative charges one finds in atomic structure; but the analogy is probably superficial. One explanation undoubtedly lies in the fact that an apparatus is composed of and relies on men who are driven by self-interest and avarice as well as by idealism; indeed, their egoism

35

and ambition is one of the reasons for their success within an apparatus. However organized, there is a quality of personal and human competition for power. The centrally attractive idea to men purely ambitious is chiefly a means of furthering their interest: of itself, the idea has little interest. Indeed, not infrequently, the men of the apparatus consider the central conception as designed to secure the acquiescence of others, but not as a principle of action of the men of the apparatus themselves.

Further, and for quite understandable motives, the coherence and strength of the apparatus is of more interest to the men operating it than the attainment of the abstract ideal. Rarely does it happen that men leading an organization will sacrifice the organization and their position with it to attain the abstract ideal for which it was organized. This is by no means necessarily discreditable. Loss of the organization or apparatus means necessarily loss of power to make gains towards the ideal in future—certainly by political processes.

Actually, the apparatus constantly seeks to dominate the formulation of the central conception in any manner which contributes strength to the apparatus itself, and to the power of the men operating it. In consequence, what was originally an endeavor to create an apparatus to realize an ideal, tends inevitably, perhaps insensibly, to become an endeavor to formulate an ideal in any terms that will add to the power of individuals.

The importance of this antithesis between the human motives of men constituting an apparatus and the realization of the central ideal cannot be exaggerated. It is crucial. This probably is the active truth behind Lord Acton's famous aphorism concerning the corrupting quality of power. Not often in history do managers of a political apparatus foresee this with the clarity shown by the statesmen who handled the affairs of the American Revolution. These men, many of them first-rate political philosophers, worked out the system of "checks and balances" which appear in the Constitution of the United States, at least partly to prevent the apparatus from strangling the democratic ideal.

Though the historical evidence is far from complete, a theory may be hazarded here. Where the force of the apparatus and the force of the central ideal are in balance, the political force created tends to be stable—that is, to survive. Where they are out of balance, the political force tends to disintegrate. Either it becomes a nonpolitical movement, depending merely on intellectual and moral acceptance of the ideal without political implementation; or the apparatus throttles the central ideal, becoming a naked power mechanism doomed eventually to break up for want of a central nucleus. An ideal without apparatus certainly has a place in the world; but it is not a political force. An apparatus based on personalities seeking and defending power only, tends to be short-lived, breaking up at length because of its own internal animosities, and of its lack of ability to command acquiescence.

§6

The process of selection becomes observable at this stage in the growth of a revolutionary political force.

An apparatus, particularly in its extreme form, such as a totalitarian dictatorship, appears to develop a central thesis distinct from the moral values affirmed or claimed by the revolution itself. Power, it seems, must justify itself; and, for some reason which perhaps we need not here seek, power commonly seeks justification not merely as a means of realizing the moral values affirmed but also on other grounds. Possibly the moral values which served the ideological base for a revolution are themselves incompatible with the continuance of dictatorship: this has been true in several cases. True or not, a separate ideology commonly does develop around dictatorial power; and the longer the dictatorial power continues, the greater is the tendency to justify that power by a thesis diverging from the thesis justifying the original revolution. To this is due the fact that revolutions are so commonly betrayed. Three illustrations may be given, two of them familiar in our own times, and one of them a short span of history ago.

The German Revolution of 1933 which brought Hitler into power claimed as its central thesis the restoration of order, employment, and economic benefit to Germany. As its apparatus, it chose force, intimidation, and the doctrine of German rights as a master race. Once established, the dictatorship discarded or rather regarded as merely incidental the earlier promising of order and economic advancement, undertaking instead to develop as underlying ideology the right of Germans to rule the world in the name of a locally created "hero" or Fuehrer by military conquest and Germanic penetration. To give this core of ideas greater sanction, a "religion" was even invented—

the worship of Wotan and the service of the Sword. The earlier ideology had been a clearly traceable, corrupt version of Marxian economic doctrine, from which indeed Hitler had derived most of his earlier ideas. But by the time Hitler was firmly established in the German saddle, he and his associates had evolved out of the Nazi apparatus a quite separate group of notions, whose central thesis was that of a "universal empire," grounded solidly on the right of German racialists to rule the world because of their self-proclaimed innate physical, mental, and moral superiority. It remains a mystery how the collection of indiscriminate balderdash found in *Mein Kampf*, added to the still more absurd nonsense grafted on to it through Rosenberg's invented religion, Haushofer's invented geopolitics, and Darré's economics of slave labor, could serve as a nucleus for any serious political force. Yet the fact is that this amazing ideology did hold a political force together for the better part of twelve years. The original centrally attractive thesis of the revolution had, of course, been discarded.

In historical fact, a selection had taken place. A bad selection, as eventually appeared.

Somewhat the same process appears to have taken place in the Russian Revolution. The difficulty of communication, and relative absence of material makes it difficult to speak with certainty. Yet indications there are sufficient to demonstrate that the process is going ineluctably forward. The original concept of the Russian Revolution is, of course, thoroughly documented; Lenin's theses of 1918 were based squarely on the economic and social doctrines of Marx and Engels, to which Lenin added his own doctrine (it is, indeed, his chief contribution) of the tactic and technique of class war throughout the world. On this compound of Marxian ideology and his own tactical apparatus, Lenin built the Russian Revolution. It is fair to observe that during his lifetime he adhered to this doctrine without major change, though even he shifted ground to some extent. His successor, Stalin, prior to becoming Chief of State, had propounded a variant: the Marxian-Leninist program could be successfully carried out within a single country such as Soviet Russia, that is, could be realized by a species of nationalism. Stalin having attained power in his turn, one after another new idea comes into the picture, pushing out the original concept. One of these is Pan-Slavism—the unity of all Slavic races—nothing new in Russian history. To the theory of a universal social revolution there was now added the substantially inconsistent idea of an all-Slavic bloc—an empire in everything but name. It would not be surprising to find—and there are already indications—that with this goes a conviction of Slavic race-superiority. This, in fact, is already appearing in the form of a doctrine, frequently repeated, that only Slavs can really understand Communism, and therefore are entitled to lead a Communist-dominated world. Still a third idea was the recrudescence of an old Czarist claim that Russia, as inheritor of the chief body of Greek Orthodox Catholics, has somehow become the heir of the old Greco-Roman Empire, that great Byzantine territory of which Constantinople was for centuries the capital. What appears to be occurring is a steady integration into the idea of the socialist state of Russian nationalism and race-superiority, extended to the ends of the earth. You find it even on the streets of American cities, where affiliates of an All-Slav Congress directed from Moscow urge Slav racial and national solidarity in chapters in Pittsburgh, Chicago, and Cleveland. It is a far cry from this sort of thing, with its militarist apparatus, back to the original nucleus of ideas bringing about the social revolution which reached power in October, 1917.

The third illustration is familiar to everyone. The nuclear concept of the French Revolution was, of course, that of the rights of man, the social contract, limitation of the power of the state, and freedom of the individual from interference by tyrants, kings, and nobles. It was a conception of individualist freedom. In the space of a decade, a different ideology, that of the glory of France and Napoleon, inspired the political and military apparatus as French Revolutionary armies scored victory after victory over their enemies and extended their conquests of "liberation," setting up puppet republics in their wake. In full flower, Napoleon bluntly and forthrightly discarded the ideology of the French Revolution. He quite frankly and steadily undertook to legitimate himself, and through himself, the nationalist position of France.

Again over a space of years there had been a selection. As one result the Napoleonic political force which met the armies of Europe on the field at Leipsic in 1812, and again on the field of Waterloo, was almost totally different from the revolutionary force which beat back France's European neighbors on the battlefield of Valmy.

41

So today, if war should come between the western powers and the Soviet Union—a war which every sane American must hope will never come—the political force represented by the Kremlin would be vastly different from that which gave battle in 1919 when Lloyd George, Clemenceau, and Woodrow Wilson sent troops to try to break the Russian Revolution in the Caucasus, the Ukraine, and the Baltic countries. The Russia which liberated Poland and the Baltic Republics in the name of the social revolution expressed a quite different political force from that of the government which has seized Bulgaria, Rumania, Poland, Hungary, and Czechoslovakia and a number of others in the name of Soviet security and Slavic supremacy.

§7

This selection of a new central thesis, nuclear to governments set up by revolution, perhaps will help to explain a familiar phenomenon.

Almost without exception, revolutionary governments in their maturity become imperialist. Certainly the liberal revolution of Cromwell found itself in its later phases proponent of the bloodiest warfares and conquests, including the subjugation of Ireland. Certainly the wars of the Reformation began by affirming the right to dissent from the Catholic religion, and ended by becoming indiscriminate struggles between various princes for greater territory and power. Undeniably the French Revolution to secure the Rights of Man in its late phase gave birth to one of the greatest imperialist drives history had seen up to that moment, causing the creation of a transient Napoleonic Empire. Certainly the Fascist and Nazi revolutions in Italy and Germany, once firmly established, reached out at once for empire. It is impossible to escape the conclusion that the Soviet Union is doing the same thing today.

Even the American Revolution of 1776 is less an exception than appears. At the close of the administration of John Adams a plot was apparently being developed in the American high command (under General Wilkinson) for seizure of the adjacent Spanish territory of Louisiana. Hamilton dreamed of something like this; Aaron Burr actually hatched a plan to drop down the Mississippi and filibuster an expedition to seize New Orleans. Temporarily, this hazy trend to expansion stopped with the election of Jefferson though probably the force behind it was far from spent. In any case, by a stroke of historical fortune, in 1803 Jefferson was able to acquire without war the huge, empty territory of Louisiana. At once the young republic began to settle and occupy this territory, expending its imperialist drive in the constructive work of settlement without having to indulge the cost of purely imperialist conquest. The push left the United States with an idea that it was somehow entitled to most of the continent of North America; a doctrine of "Manifest Destiny" remained as a legacy from that period.

§8

The conclusion can be simply stated.

At the center of every political force is a nuclear conception—a centrally attractive idea or group of ideas.

Around this nucleus there is grouped an apparatus organizing the abstraction into a political force. This apparatus may be mild, as in the case of a democratic political party, or extreme, as in the case of an oligarchy, a military system, or a police state.

There is antithesis between the apparatus and the nuclear conception. Where the apparatus is weak, the nuclear conception tends to break it down and the political force tends to disintegrate into a collection of individuals acting independently.

Where the apparatus is strong and particularly where it is extreme, the apparatus tends to modify or discard the original nuclear ideas, importing others which seem more advantageous to the apparatus itself.

Revolution, as one of the extreme manifestations of political force, tends to create an extreme apparatus commonly engendering oligarchic or dictatorial absolutism, accompanied by militarism. This in turn and of itself causes the discarding of the nuclear conception which gave the revolution birth; and new ideology is substituted. The result is a new political force, frequently using words and dialectic of the original conception, but having a quite different content. The apparatus has made a selection of ideas.

The revolution thus becomes a new, or at least a different, political force.

As this new force meets or competes with other political forces, selection has to be made between political forces.

Political history is in considerable part a record of the selections made between political forces, and the results of such selections.

The Results of Selection between Political Forces

II

The Results of Selection between Political Forces

§1

Historians will write of the mid-twentieth century period as an era of war and revolution. Our span of years takes rank with the late eighteenth cenury, and the first-half of the seventeenth century, which comprised the combined wars and upheavals respectively of the French Revolution and the Reformation. In all three periods, revolutions proposed themselves as political forces, and vast numbers of men were compelled to select between the newly appearing political forces and older ones already in existence.

These revolutions understood, apparently, the importance of a nuclear thesis. The French Revolution coined a word intended to describe it: the word "ideology." The word has survived and is used by the Communist Parties now.

The word, in its present import, was a revolutionary product. Its wide use is probably ascribable to Napoleon. He, a severely practical soul, finally liquidated the accumulated doctrine of the French Revolution with a soul-searing contempt, dismissing it in ridicule as "ideology"—a collection of dogma, not grounded in practical self-interest. An epithet of ridicule, however, as often as not solidifies a

conception. "Ideology," as a method of political action, re-
fused to remain quietly on the Napoleonic scrap-heap. In
point of fact, throughout the entire nineteenth century the
concept of struggle, based on formulated doctrine, grew in
strength. Indeed one of the most dangerous aspects of today's world-division lies precisely in the fact that the two
principal ideologies now struggling for supremacy are
both more than a century old—both probably approaching obsolescence in the light of the twentieth-century
knowledge—both outdated.

Ideology, in present political jargon, is a doctrine
united to a "dialectic," the word used to denote the justification of the apparatus. The latter is perhaps the significant evolution. As we have seen, a doctrine, however appealing, rarely becomes a political force unless it is united
to an apparatus of persuasion by which it entices, attracts,
cajoles, intimidates, coerces or terrorizes, masses of people
into acceptance. Dialectic, in the modern political sense,
is a word often applied now to the entire apparatus—intellectual, political, economic and perhaps even military.

In its earlier, more respectable sense, dialectic was a
method of argument, of search for truth amid conflicting
evidence; a purely intellectual process. Today, unhappily,
the use has widened. If conversion to any body of doctrine
is desirable, say the realists, then any means, however gross,
to effect that conversion may be comprehended within dialectic. The means and the ends are fused into a single body
of thinking; and the "ideology" comes to comprehend not
merely the underlying doctrine, but also the entire range
of accepted methods by which it is to be made powerful.

48

Remembering, as we do, the tremendous range of propaganda, of "political warfare," of stimulation of mass action, used more or less by all belligerents in wartime and particularly in World War II, it can be surmised that a modern Napoleon would be less cavalier in disregarding "ideologies." Oppose them he might; ignore them, he certainly could not. More likely, as Stalin, Hitler, Mussolini, the National Association of Manufacturers or the Ku Klux Klan have done, he would seize and operate an "ideology" (dialectic included) as a major instrument of power.

Nevertheless, even today, "ideology" does furnish the basis on which men choose or select between one political force and another. It is the mass of statement, often confused and sometimes contradictory, of the essence of the centrally attractive nucleus. It is the kit of statements, exposition, and what-not offered to the masses, and the dialectic is supposed to furnish added motivation causing them to select the nuclear thesis thus offered.

In this essay, we shall try to study certain great selections between competing political forces.

The existence of these selections is part of recorded history. So also are their results. The endeavor here made is to show that the result proceeded necessarily from the selection made.

§2

Here we must leave to the philosopher, to the moralist, his function of endeavoring to determine the ethical, abstract "good." This writer is clear that as our knowledge becomes greater we shall discover that this apparent abstraction, which we now set aside, is by no means irrelevant—that a political force tends to be permanent in direct ratio as it tends to approach in central thesis and in the principles of its apparatus the abstract "good."

But this lies ahead. For the present let us take a harsher rule of judgment.

Let us consider that a "good" political force is that force which demonstrates that it can survive and maintain itself—which necessarily includes the fact that it enables its followers, its adherents, the nations it organizes and international groups it brings into being, to survive likewise. A "bad" force is a force which leads its followers—local, national, or international—towards defeat, dispersal, and, at the extreme, towards destruction.

In politics, as in nature, it is apparently possible to select an organization of life which, though temporarily successful, leads eventually towards extinction. The natural selection of species is strewn with extinct forms of life which had selected a mechanism temporarily adequate to conditions but defenseless in the end against circumstances. The Brontosaurs protected themselves by bulk; the sabre-toothed tiger by brute ferocity; the Neanderthal Man, by size and reliance on a single weapon—the club. Each in time, limited by the selected form, disappeared under the attack of species inferior in these qualities but better able to comprehend and deal with the totality of circumstances. A famous French scientist, Dr. Alexis Carrel, who was interested in applying some of these lessons to contemporary man, generalized his conclusions by saying that adaptability, rather than specific, predetermined defense or offense, was the quality which leads to animal survival. He reasoned accordingly that in the case of modern man, the qualities most likely to lead to survival were the qualities making men adaptable to the widest possible range of circumstances.

Study of the life and death of political forces would be the work of a lifetime. As an experiment in testing our hypothesis, two instances are chosen for our laboratory experiment. The first is concerned with the situation existing at the end of the world wars precipitated by the French Revolution. They were closed by the Treaty of Vienna in 1815, presenting Europe with a choice, and occasioning a selection of political forces, occasioning results which we must examine. The second is the somewhat comparable situation resulting at the termination of World War I, formally ended by the Treaty of Versailles. Again the selection of political force was made; again we have a more or less measurable estimate of the results.

§3

The French revolutionaries, whether philosophers or mob leaders, successfully challenged in 1793 the whole conception of the king-state. They rejected the conception of a divinely ordained monarch, advancing civilization through the achievements of his court even as he extended his dominions and transmitted his culture through the might of his arms. "The powers of Europe would challenge us," said Danton after the execution of Louis XVI. "We throw them the head of a king." Instead, the thesis of equal participation of all men in political life carried forward by the apparatus of a republican state with more or less recognizable political parties had begun to make its way. Napoleon had made himself heir to this; but instead of consolidating around the original central thesis, he had reverted to the idea and apparatus of the king-state. At the close of his career he so nearly approximated both the conception and the apparatus of his opponents that there was substantial support for a plan to retain him on the throne of France.

It is true that at Vienna, the representatives of the assembled Powers paid relatively little attention to self-analysis. Only the ablest among them took account of the French Revolution. Few realized the depth of the impression it had made. One can imagine a modern analyst ferried back a century and a half, endeavoring to explain to the assembled plenipotentiaries and kings what we now know to have happened.

He would have told them that the conception of human equality in political affairs had established itself throughout the length and breadth at least of Western Europe. He would have pointed out that the defeat of the Napoleonic Empire was precisely the defeat of the Empire, and not at all the defeat of the Revolution. The Revolution, indeed, had never been defeated on the field of battle, still less in the field of purely ideological conflict. He would have demonstrated that the Frenchman, the German, the Austrian, the Englishman, the North Italian, were in no sense the same individuals who had faithfully served as feudal serfs or peasants on the estates of a noble owner. He would have explained that the intellectuals, the professional men, the tradesmen, merchants, and similar manufacturers of the towns no longer thought in the same terms as their predecessors in the days of Marie Antoinette. He would have agreed that the progress of the revolutionary ideas as they then were was uneven throughout Europe, but that it was great, and growing. He would have concluded by pointing out that the content of a restored king-state in 1815 was and continued to be almost completely different from the content of that same king-state a generation earlier.

Had he been convinced of the hypothesis we are here examining, he would have pointed out that the assembled statesmen had now to choose the central core of ideas on which political forces in Europe were to be erected. Would they be organizing their states to express this growing equality of individuals in political matters, though in orderly organization? Or would they endeavor to re-establish the *status quo* as it stood before the battle of Valmy, and reconstruct the hierarchic nationalist state, expressed through an absolute king who concentrated in himself feudal privileges? On this choice of ideologic nucleus, to be surrounded by the apparatus of the prevailing nationalism of the time, the history of Europe might ultimately hang.

We can be sure that had our anachronistic visitor talked in such terms, he would hardly have been understood by most of the assembly. To most of the men there—not all—a horrid revolutionary force had emerged, and had reached its logical result by producing a ferocious aggressor, against whom the European world had united in justifiable defense. To them Bonaparte had led the revolutionary force to ultimate defeat. In this view the semi-feudal king-state with its nuclear idea of nationalism and its apparatus of national machinery was the normal, pre-tested order of things. Re-establish, get back to normal; life will resume a path from which it was merely temporarily diverted! As clever a man as Metternich observed that what the people wanted was not liberty but order. King-states could certainly provide that, especially if they could arrange among themselves to keep the peace. And Europe selected for the moment the nuclear idea of nationalism, and the apparatus of the king-state as a political force. As it proved, Europe selected a weak force which did not survive.

For, underlying and pervading the European system set up by the Treaty of Vienna, there remained the developing conception of the French Revolution. It had been ousted from its apparatus when discarded by Napoleon, and the apparatus, surviving the betrayal of the idea, had now been crushed in military defeat. As Dr. Alvin Johnson put it: "The one net gain was the advance in international reach and social understanding that had been created by the thinkers." Yet that gain, modest perhaps, was widely dispersed. French intellectuals did not cease to exist because Louis XVIII once more presided over a Bourbon court in Paris. True, they were not welcome at that court—but, for that matter, neither had they been intimate at the court of Napoleon. The Revolutionary intellectuals, for example Madame de Staël and her great companion Benjamin Constant, had been a nuisance to the French Empire.

("That woman is a pest!" Napoleon had exclaimed.) A generation had grown up with an entirely new and general idea of participation in politics. There was no way of checking this ruinous participation.

In Germany the change was equally great. In 1777 a German Prince, the Landgrave of Hesse, like other German Princes conscripted the able-bodied men of his realm into an army, and sold that army as mercenaries to other Princes for so much on the hoof. George III of England used them with moderate effectiveness against the American Revolution. In the Napoleonic Wars, young Germans had been inspired to rise against their more or less tyrannous masters (possibly a great play, *Intrigue and Love*, by the famous German poet Schiller, had helped this along). As happens with all too terrible frequency when young men revolt, they found themselves not martyrs in a cause, but pawns in a betrayed revolution. The armies they joined became units in Napoleon's imperial forces, whereby it came about that the great majority of troops with which he invaded Russia in 1812 were not French. But young men do learn, even from betrayed revolutions; and these organized clandestinely in a German underground which later became the army of liberation against Napoleon. They were hardly likely to accept anew the status of "dumb driven cattle" imposed by the German Princes on their fathers a generation past.

And so throughout great parts of Europe. The nuclear ideas of the French Revolution were not nationalist, they were universal. They had a wide degree of application, whether the words were spoken by Jefferson in Philadelphia in 1776, or by Robespierre in the French National Assembly, or by the British liberals, or by the propagandists of whom Napoleon made full use in his far-flung campaigns, or by the European republicans after Waterloo.

The history of the generation after Vienna is the record of the fate of the political force chosen by ruling statesmen not too closely in contact with their peoples. Chosen badly, if short life is a test. In the following years every university-bred student group talked a language which did not correspond with the conception of the absolute king-state, and resisted its police apparatus. What remained of the counter-Imperial popular movements ("undergrounds" we should call them today), simply declined to be written off. A German group, the *Burschenschaft* or youth movement, became so obstreperous that on Metternich's advice it was eventually dissolved; but it celebrated its demise with a popular song which was familiar in Germany even during my own lifetime. Defenders of Metternich insist that in Austria he urged some advance towards the new conception upon his master, the Austrian Emperor, and maintain that Metternich's failure to secure more enlightened measures on the part of the Austrian court was due to inability to act rather than lack of appreciation of the forces involved. Perhaps; but Metternich's devotion to the imperial royalist apparatus must have obscured his views upon ideology.

The fact was that the apparatus of king-state operation surrounded a conception and an ideology in which few educated men had faith.

Worse yet, apparatus and conception alike began to

look ridiculous against the background of the emergent Industrial Revolution. The king-state, heir to feudalism, had a certain logic in dealing with the economics of countries devoted to agriculture, defended by old-style, land armies. A medieval count could function as combined peace-giver and landowner, especially if he had the brains to choose able bailiffs. But a belted earl, or a well-scutcheoned duke as head of a cloth factory, or manager of one of these new-fangled railroads, simply looked funny. Mark Twain, writing *A Connecticut Yankee at King Arthur's Court*, has a couple of sardonic chapters on the Yankee's attempt to make knights into railway conductors, and on King Arthur's attempt to choose officers of a technical army in accordance with the blueness of their blood. The pervasive, applicable forces in the new Europe under Metternich were no longer the great noblemen, nor even the kings. They were the rising financial barons, like the Rothschilds; men who were able to master a moderate amount of mechanical engineering; people who could make use of the new giant of steam; people who could appeal to men's minds by talking and writing, instead of issuing edicts whose authority came from divine right or inherited titular possession. This was more than a mere moral threat to the king-state; it was a material threat as well. Actual maintenance of the state whether as an economic or a military unit, depended on its being able to command the services of just such people. And there was always present the disturbing example of a young republic called the United States which was, incomprehensibly, making an astonishing success of itself.

As the nuclear ideas of Magna Carta had done before, the disembodied nuclear ideas of the French Revolution presently took on new apparatus. Political parties grew up, and insisted on the institution of legislatures, representing the people, chosen through enlarged franchise. These party-apparatuses acted through agitation, organization, and mass movements of greater or less strength. Intellectuals wrote and talked. Others agitated. Political leaders of greater or less strength appeared on street corners.

In one case, Britain, the genius of a nation asserted itself, recognized the new political force, and without violence accepted the new conception. The political fact was substantially accomplished by the Reform Bill of 1832, and its successor reforms. H. G. Wells observed that, in the nineteenth-century revolutionary age, the great achievement of England was that it did *not* have a revolution—but absorbed the content of the new conception and peaceably adapted the apparatus of the old state. France was less fortunate: barricades went up in the streets of Paris in 1830; a new king took over largely because he publicly subscribed to the ideals of the French Revolution —and because his father, Philippe Egalité, a Bourbon Prince, had voted to behead Louis XVI.

What Metternich later called the "preface to revolution" was fairly begun.

Nor did it end. For eighteen years, a series of revolutionary movements battered at the weakening political forces of the king-states. They raised problems curiously like those which occupy the headlines of the newspapers of our own time. Greece: and freedom of the Greek population from the Turkish Empire through which no Greek could hope to obtain effective political expression. Italy, then a geographic expression only, where Italians sought to establish their right to make political history in place of a sorry collection of foreign kings, archdukes, and grand dukes who ruled a string of rickety states. Germany: was she to be unified, as a nationally conscious people, or divided, as the property of a historical collection of royal and princely families?

To Metternich, a poised, polished, and powerful figure, who by skill and diplomacy directed the affairs of Europe, all this was terribly dangerous. He had found a formula for keeping the peace—a formula based on the similarity of interests of the monarchs of king-states and especially of their kings. From it he created the outline of a European state: the Concert of Powers. Eliminate this, he reasoned, and you take out the single method evolved by which Europe can be kept at peace. And in this regard he was right—if the only interest worth saving in the world was peace-keeping. His ghost would point out that the popular states whose creation he fought made a far poorer record of keeping out of war than Metternich's Concert of Powers. But essentially Metternich's formula was peace without freedom; peace without popular participation in politics; and the flowing tide ran sheer and turgid towards the Revolution of 1848.

§4

There is not space here to analyze the Revolution of 1848, relevant though it would be. It is said to have failed.

The verdict is hardly accurate. In it were contained the tragedies common to most revolutions. A popular rising in France sought another Bonaparte—and was again betrayed by a Bonaparte. There was the frustrated struggle in Spain; the liberation of Greece, less by British diplomacy than by British liberals. At length, the passionate day in Vienna with a mob calling for the retirement of Metternich—and his final surrender.

Only in retrospect can we disentangle from the multitude of events the main forces which were establishing themselves.

The political force of the king-state had played—had played a losing hand well, in the main, as the survival of Napoleon III, of the Hohenzollerns, of the Russian tsars, and of the Austrian House of Hapsburg plainly attested. But, establishing itself in almost equal strength, was the new, liberal force built around the conception of popular participation in political affairs and assuming the apparatus of democratic nationalism. "Self-determination," Woodrow Wilson was to christen it later. For the time, it was a sound choice. Nationalism, which we deprecate today, at that time undoubtedly offered a vehicle by which popular participation—democracy—could find greater expression. The north Italian youth revolted against a Bourbon prince or Hapsburg grand duke because he wished to become a citizen participating in political affairs. Creation of Italy as a strong and effective nation offered him just that possibility. The apparatus of Italian nationalism gave effective form to this individualist democratic conception.

At the Congress of Vienna, Europe had recreated the

system of king-states, ignoring the democratic idea-content of the French Revolution. Europe had selected—and the selection was imperfect.

Certain qualities of the idea-content selected made for survival when choice was made of the king-state conception: it had ability, for the time being, to maintain order; and, in the main, to keep peace. But conception and apparatus of the king-state also had qualities which made for destruction: it excluded newly enfranchised politically conscious people from participation in affairs; it was inadaptable to modern economics and mechanics; it made for spiritual frustration of intellectuals, students, youth. The negatives outbalanced the positives. The king-state, though it survived the Revolution of 1848 in form, was fatally wounded. Full measure of adherence to that political force in fact doomed the people thus adhering to deterioration, and indeed, to possible destruction, as the Gods of History were to show.

For one must note the fact that the three states which most closely adhered to the king-state formula of the conference of Vienna were Russia, under the Romanov tsars, Germany under the Hohenzollerns, and Austria under the Hapsburgs. These were, in fact, the cornerstones of the Concert of Powers. But in 1918, just a century after Talleyrand, Metternich, and Castlereagh recognized them as dominant modes, all king-state empires, idea, apparatus and all, exploded in a cloud of historical dust blown up by World War I.

At Vienna, in 1815, the men in control of the governments of Europe made a selection, and had enforced it on

their peoples. In 1848, a new choice was possible: half
Europe selected the newer force of democratic nationalism; the other half adhered to the king-state. In 1948 no
European king-states existed; and the people that adhered
to them have been successfully shattered, and have been
taken over by other political forces.

In historical perspective, the case for the king-state was
perhaps arguable at Vienna. In 1848, the choice of it was
simply "bad"; bad in the deadly sense that, as a political
force, the king-state and those adhering to it were doomed
to disappear.

§5

Though history rarely, if ever, repeats itself, its drama
often repeats an old theme in a different key. It is here suggested that the pattern of selection of political force we
have traced for the nineteenth century is repeating itself
in this, our more turbulent twentieth.

Let us begin with the year 1919. The city is Paris, not
Vienna. The king-state, Germany, allied to another king-
state, Austro-Hungary, had failed to keep the peace with
the third surviving king-state—Russia. Peace-keeping had
been the great merit asserted for them in the age of Metternich; and they had failed to keep peace. A world war resulted. At its conclusion, all three of these states were
smashed to fragments. Again the victorious powers were
meeting to discuss peace—which then, as now, had for its
primary task the reconstitution of Europe.

The victor states, of which the United States was now
one, were all nations which had embraced and practiced
democratic nationalism, the precise revolutionary political

force opposed by Metternich. They were organized around the liberal conception of popular participation in government; their apparatus was that of democratic organization. France, Britain, the United States—and to a lesser extent, Italy—were the triumphant heirs of a "good" choice of political force.

In considerable measure, the nuclear idea of democratic nationalism had been restated with precision and eloquence in the war speeches of an American President, Woodrow Wilson. Glistening phrases, "self-determination of nations" and a "world safe for democracy," lay in the consciousness of every European. Peace-keeping was believed to be inherent in this conception: Wilson had argued, eloquently, that democratic nations are never aggressors. The Fourteen Points interpreted in this sense constituted a square proposal that the Paris Peace Conference, on behalf of the world, choose liberal democracy as its centrally attractive thesis, and democratically controlled nationalist states as apparatus. Here was a splendid vindication of the political forces which had been ignored at Vienna, had struggled to limited victories in 1848, and which now appeared as ruling the world.

But was this all? For another political force had come into action: the Communist Revolution in Russia. Whereas democratic nationalism appealed to and tended to satisfy men's desire to participate on a more or less equal basis in political affairs, Communist materialism now proposed the thesis that all men should participate on a more or less equal basis in economic affairs. Freedom might satisfy the soul; but only food satisfies the stomach. Democratic nationalism, according to the Marxian theory, was merely an apparatus by which the trader, speculator, bourgeois, and capitalist could displace the king and the nobles. Its talk of freedom was claimed to be an insincere sham. Neither the capitalist nor the king, said these new voices, was prepared to admit the common people to an equal place in enjoyment of land, of production, of distribution, of standards of living. In the rigid, stratified, class system of Europe, the argument looking towards equal economic participation had tremendous force: such force indeed that its adherents were prepared to sacrifice political rights to obtain a dictatorship in the interest of the proletariat—provided the economic dream were realized. Without an approach to economic equality, said they, theoretical rights in politics—or in thought—are meaningless. There is, they claimed, merely an illusion of political freedom—men are bound in slavery to wages, slavery to irrational economic fluctuations, slavery to markets. Economic determination rules society; Marxian economics must be the regnant ideology. This conception had mustered an apparatus, Lenin being its principal architect, and it had proved capable of seizing the Russian Empire. Its adherents were governing the mutilated European Russia which emerged as World War I ended. Thus the Communists.

But the Communists were doing more. They were active in the wreckage of the former king-state of Germany. Civil war waged by their faction washed into Berlin, which, even as the Paris Peace Conference debated, was divided by barbed-wire barricades and anguished by bloody streets. A Communist political force was powerfully represented and briefly triumphant in Hungary, now in process of separation from the king-state of Austria. In lesser force, Communist apparatuses were active elsewhere. They were challenging the victorious forces of democratic nationalism, somewhat as the remnants of the French Revolution at Vienna challenged the victorious king-states of a century ago.

It is fascinating—and not pleasant—to remember that the democratic nationalists at the Versailles Peace Conference reacted towards all this much as Metternich and the Congress of Vienna had reacted towards the democratic republicans of their time. Specifically, the Versailles Conference authorized the invasion of Russia through several fronts: by the British from the north, and indirectly, through the Caucasus; by the French from the Black Sea littoral and in the Ukraine. The United States briefly entered the picture by sending a regiment to Archangel, and by occupying Vladivostock.

There occurred a tiny ripple within the Conference itself. A number of younger men in various delegations, chiefly American and British, considered that it might be possible to find common ground, or at least peace, between two conceptions which are not, after all, mutually exclusive. Intellectually at least it appears possible to unite a high degree of economic equality with a high degree of individual political participation in free democratic government. At all events, it should be possible for the two conceptions to co-exist. At least two attempts were made to bring about a meeting of the forces. The first resulted in arrangements for a parley between the victorious powers present in Paris, and the representatives of the Russian Soviets. A time was fixed for the Conference, and a place: Prince's Isle, in the Sea of Marmora near Constantinople. Though lip-service was paid to the idea, the powerful French delegation objected, intrigued against it, took advice from Russian *émigrés,* and in the end the project foundered on Clemenceau's opposition. A second, British-American, attempt worked up by Col. House and Sir Philip Kerr (later Lord Lothian) resulted in sending a young American, William C. Bullitt, to Moscow to negotiate a treaty of understanding. The treaty was easily obtained by him; but again opposition within the Allied ranks caused him to be disowned by Lloyd George, quietly dropped by Wilson, and prevented serious consideration, on the Allied side, of that or any other treaty with the Communist government of Russia.

Instead, Woodrow Wilson, Clemenceau, and Lloyd George reconsidered. They determined in May of 1919 that the time had come for decisive overthrow of the Communist republic. They gave instruction to draw documents recognizing an anti-Communist army and counterrevolutionary government headed by Admiral Kolchak, who had crossed Siberia and was invading European Russia through the Ural Mountains. This was surprising to say the least, since intelligence reports showed that Admiral Kolchak had already been decisively defeated near the Volga valley, and was falling back into Siberia as rapidly as he could. But this information did not change the decision of the Big Three; the recognition went through; and the Allies formally backed the counterrevolution. Disrespectfully, the Soviet armies caught up with Admiral Kolchak at Lake Baikal, defeated him there, and shot him out of hand. The chance to find common ground between the two conceptions had, of course, disappeared for the time.

§6

The decades following the Treaty of Versailles signed in 1919 resemble somewhat the decades following the Congress of Vienna. Yet there is a difference.

The liberal conception of democratic nationalism is by its nature capable of absorbing new economic forms. This is one of its greatest merits. Democratic procedure and popular participation offer precisely that opportunity—partly because they refuse to accept, as we have seen, the extreme apparatus of dictatorship, with accompanying denial of civil rights, machinery of a police state, and strangulation of the central concept. Leninist Communism as a political force has no such absorptive quality. In many, perhaps most, respects Leninism is more rigid even than the old king-state. It cannot absorb: it must conquer; it must liquidate where it cannot convert. Possibly conscious of this, the Leninist of today makes a religion of his rigidity, and even has his dialectic poets write hymns to the glory of the secret police. A liberal democrat can look objectively at the tenets of Communism and learn from them. It is of the essence of the Leninist conception that it has nothing to learn from the outside, and that it cannot be objective about anything.

The facts indicate, indeed, that the nuclear conception of the Communist Revolution has already been strangled by its own apparatus, just as philosophical democracy was shattered by Napoleon's. The issues presenting themselves to us appear, in present perspective, to be more nearly like the problem presented to Europe in 1807 than in 1847. In 1807 Napoleon, riding the French Revolution, had become as great an enemy of philosophical democracy as the feudal king-states who opposed him. Today the conception of more or less equal opportunity and economic participation —the attractive heart of the original Communist ideology —is far better expressed in Scandinavia or the United States than in Russia itself, judging by results.

§7

Have we the right to endeavor to foretell the future from the experiments of the past? It is not part of our given task. If the writer were attempting it, he would prophesy that the Russian Communists' imperial drive, and its apparatus of police-state, armies, and hierarchic dictatorship, with or without war, will eventually be crushed as surely as was the Napoleonic Empire; and that the greatest wisdom of the Kremlin would be to recognize that inevitability, and change course. But the crushing of an apparatus of political power is not the crushing of an idea. Metternich remarked in the last century: "The effect of revolution never is obliterated—never." Striving towards greater participation and more equal benefit in economics would not die, even if the Soviet Union were defeated and dismembered. That concept, which has universal appeal, and which does not depend on ultra-imperialism and police-dictatorship, is likely to remain as an in-

68

fluential idea long after the world has disposed of the current Communist apparatus and the Soviet police-state.

Then (or more accurately, "now" as we prepare for "then"), the selection which is slowly taking place at this time may be apparent. Unquestionably the choice again lies between two major political forces, and is being made between them. One is nationalist political democracy, with substantial modification of the old economic system. The other is dictatorial force professing economic equalitarianism. There is, perhaps, opportunity for a newer and greater Metternich to bring the best of economic ideology into the political force of democratic nationalism; to do on an international scale what British statesmanship was able to do in 1832 when it reconciled political democracy with the king-state and paved the way for Britain's greatest century. And there is opportunity for a great Communist statesman to liberate the individual within the new economic frame he has made. Were both opportunities seized, we should have peace in our time.

Or the selection may be through other and less intelligent, more costly or more bloody means. But selection there will surely be—and the lives of peoples depend on the choice.

§8

We began by recognizing the penomenon of political forces in social affairs. We followed by posing the fact of continuous and continuing selection by peoples among rival political forces. In this rough examination we have glanced at a few spectacular cases of political force, and at certain selections which have taken place.

We suggested that political forces may be classified as "good" or "bad" dependent on whether they make for survival, or for disintegration. On that basis, it becomes relevant to examine how selection is made; and why a political force in given circumstances has tended to survival, or has tended to disintegration.

If the hypothesis be accepted thus far, the historian has emerged from mere narration and description. He becomes a recorder and analyst in the infinite laboratory of human experience; his work offers material which the social scientist may analyze, and on which he may base a conclusion.

In the dim future it may become possible for peoples or politicians to select between political forces on a basis of reasonably accurate knowledge, and on moderately well-based prediction. It may be possible for a social scientist to say: "You may select this force or that; but this force means survival; that, destruction," and to give valid reasons for his conclusion. We may, in a word, begin to emerge in the political sciences from the age of alchemy and astrology, into an age corresponding in social and political matters, somewhat to the exactness of chemistry. The social scientist of the future may offer us a true vision of the orbits of distant historical stars.

The Process of Selection

III

The Process of Selection

WE HAVE dealt thus far with the structure of political force; with the fact that peoples select as between political forces; and we have noted that selection has results. It becomes necessary now to consider what "selection" actually is, and how it is achieved. For selection is a complex process. That it occurs and has results is a matter of historical fact. How it occurs, who does it, and when, is matter of speculation.

Yet the study is of first importance, particularly in a democracy like that of the United States. We stake our very existence on the theory that our people have the power, the right, and the duty to select between competing political forces. We hope to construct a community of nations working more or less on that principle. This is, to us, the essence of liberal democracy.

§1

When a political force is nascent, a preliminary selection is made by the individuals first attracted by its central thesis. This selection lies on the threshold.

It presents, essentially, only two alternatives: to create a political force by surrounding the central idea with appropriate apparatus—or to refuse to create a political force, leaving the central thesis to influence life and events by influencing the personalities and individual actions of its converts and sympathizers.

An ideal, a conception, or an ethic, may find realization through the results of a political force; and it may also achieve results through the more dispersed and multiple paths of individual conduct. A philosophy of life, interpreted by the thoughts and deeds of unorganized men and women, grounded in a central ideal, may, and indeed frequently has, become more influential in world history than the most powerful political force ever created though it forms no apparatus, seeks no power, and does not aim to choose governors.

Instances of conscious choice against erection of an ideal into political force by the men involved are not many. When they do occur, they are often unknown. But we have, in carefully recorded history, at least one amazing example of such a choice. The results of that choice have influenced history for two thousand years. The occasion was the conscious decision made by Christ on the Palm Sunday preceding his crucifixion.

Transcendental theology aside, the political facts of that famous event are fairly clear. A new and splendid spiritual conception had been unfolded in the tiny kingdom of Judea. It had attracted a mass of followers. It had engaged the attention, imagination, and hopes of thousands of people. In the Oriental world of the time practical men would assume, as a matter of course, that this vast stirring would be directed into concrete political channels. One may fairly infer, indeed, that some groups unrecorded in the Gospels and in history squarely considered and were quietly working towards just this result. Demonstrations like that which occurred on the streets of Jerusalem are

74

not usually accidental; and there is every indication that this one was well planned. An hour had been fixed; palm branches were distributed; word had been spread; the crowds were there. Some apparatus plainly was in formation.

The organizational aim of this apparatus was beginning to reach formulation. Christ had not initiated or sanctioned a claim to be "King of the Jews," but someone had thought of it, and the phrase was all over Jerusalem. This, indeed, had excited the apprehension of the Temple and the monarchy. As one reconstructs the scene, all conditions were ripe for a ringing political declaration and immediate seizure of power, in brief, for a revolution in Jerusalem on that day. Seizure of the Temple, or of the royal palace, could have happened almost at once, for the local puppet government in Judea, though carefully preserved by Roman imperial policy, had been equally carefully disarmed. A speech, a phrase, perhaps a single gesture, would have crystallized a political force capable of becoming dominant at once. The record makes it plain that no signal was given, and that the choice was deliberate.

With all reverence and without excluding other deeper religious interpretations, it seems probable that an explanation of this may fairly be found in the account of the Temptation in the wilderness. There it is told that the Devil, taking Christ to a pinnacle, offered him principalities and power—in exchange for worship. No better allegorical account could easily be given of a great spirit forced to choose between resting on spiritual force with certainty of personal catastrophe, and organizing a political force with all likelihood of temporal success. Entering the political arena with a political force, however, necessarily means limiting or denying part, at least, of the spiritual ideal. Perhaps, indeed, precisely the tenderest, most poignant, deepest and universal part. Conscious resolution that his kingdom was not "of this world" is the clearest possible statement of a decision to refuse attributes and rewards of political force in order to retain the illimitable thrust of spiritual influence.

This interpretation cannot fairly be countered by suggesting that the Roman imperial power would have prevented success of a Christian revolution. We know quite enough about Pontius Pilate to estimate his probable line of action with fair accuracy. Roman policy rather favored limited local autonomy and self-determination. A Roman governor's business was to let subject peoples run their own affairs much as they pleased, so long, of course, as they did not threaten military domination of the Roman Legions and the authority of Caesar. But Christ had said, "Render unto Caesar the things that are Ceasar's," and his moral philosophy seems to have appealed rather more to Pilate than the narrow nationalism of the Pharisees. As between accepting a new local king on the one hand, or fighting a revolt on the streets of Jerusalem on the other, Pilate's plain course was to accept the rising power with a shrug. Careful understandings would, of course, be reached with the new leader, assuring that Roman prerogatives would be respected, taxes paid, and that force should remain unchallenged in the hands of the Legions. For the rest, if the

shakeup pacified Judea, the Roman governor would be
suited. This was no revolution against him. A few days
after Palm Sunday, we find him endeavoring to release
Christ, probably moved in part by a sound political instinct that this large Christian faction ought not to be un-
duly irritated. Spiritual movements were not his business
in any case. One can perfectly imagine him diplomatically
accepting the new local regime, consolidating his own position, standing quietly by while Christ assumed leadership
of a fifth-rate Near Eastern country, becoming in name
and fact, "King of the Jews," surrounded by a puppet
court, ambitious politicians, and faced with the task of
rapidly conciliating or eliminating the defeated ecclesiastical party, as he undertook the work of governing within
the framework of Rome.

But in that moment Christianity would have died. In
exchange, a political force, probably of no great significance and doomed to a short life, would have entered the
Roman imperial scene, playing a part as brief and as
tawdry as did the Herodian monarchy. Inevitably the apparatus of the political force would have limited, dis-
credited, perhaps extinguished altogether the deep and
universal fire which conquered all Rome three centuries
later, and lights the world to this day.

When a political force is nascent, the first selection is
between the power and possibilities of an ideal, and the
power and possibilities of political action. The men who
lead at that moment may choose to take or choose to leave.
This is the first and greatest selection.

§2

More often history is concerned with selections made between political forces, tiny or great, which have already come into being. Rarely, if ever, is there complete absence of choice. Rarely, if ever, is any political force wholly without competition of some other political force. Even the most ruthless totalitarian government is commonly opposed by a counter force, though it may be underground or in exile. In time of great contention, rival political forces of similar order of magnitude are present in a given country, or group of countries, or, in these modern times, in the world at large.

How is selection then made?

In an ideal world of freedom, every individual would be politically conscious, possessed at least of the essential facts and considerations, and able to record his choice by expression or by conduct. That condition has never existed anywhere. There is, indeed, in every given case a certain number, small or great, of individuals who are politically conscious and who do choose, some on the basis of reason, more on the basis of emotion, possibly still more on the basis of personal interest. In backward and illiterate countries, the group capable of selection is tiny. Even in a great democracy like the United States it probably does not comprise more than twenty percent of the population. Below this level there is a group which chooses on the basis of personal friendships or estimates. Below them again is a greater mass which chooses almost subconsciously merely by acquiescence.

Manipulators of a political apparatus frequently aim

to reduce to a minimum the number of people capable of making conscious choice, so that selection for or against their political force must be made in terms of acquiescence or revolt. In a singularly brutal exposition of policy, Darré, one of Hitler's Ministers, explained this to a group of his collaborators at the time of the German occupation of Czechoslovakia. Every person of education, he pointed out, was to be killed, imprisoned, or otherwise disposed of. No Czechoslovakian child was to be permitted education beyond grammar school. The great bulk of Czechs were to be so placed economically that failure to acquiesce would mean starvation. Actual, formal slavery was to be instituted. Leadership from among the Czech ranks was to be made impossible. The Soviet Union has followed an exactly similar policy in its own country and those under its domination; like the Nazi state, it builds up its secret police primarily to enforce this result.

Yet there remains some fragment of selective process even under these circumstances. However ruthlessly a people is deprived of leadership, however completely it is deprived of information, man is still a reasoning animal. No method short of genocide has yet been found of eliminating the human mind from the human body. There is always an ultimate choice: choice of acquiescing in a dominant political force, or of resisting, perhaps dying. In 1948 Jan Masaryk, then Minister of Foreign Affairs of Czechoslovakia, exercised this, the only method of selection left to him, when he committed suicide rather than accept the Communist dictatorship. Thousands of others have done the same in the last five years. In the cold and inhuman judgment of history, a population which accepts a political force has "selected" it—as did the German nation when it acquiesced in the rule and work of Hitler and his Gestapo. If a great part of Germans had declined to acquiesce, Hitler's political force, encased in its Nazi apparatus, would have crumbled overnight. This is not to say that in the kindlier and more forgiving judgment which individuals may seek, those who acquiesce are "guilty." It is merely to say that the nation which acquiesces actually does select.

Here then are the extremes. Selection may be conscious, made by free men possessed of the facts. Selection may be made by ignorant or helpless people, forced to acquiesce unless they wish to undergo misery or martyrdom.

Between these extremes lie all manner of degrees. The sociology of selection is matter of study by scholars now, though quantitative scientific analysis can be carried on chiefly in areas where choice is free and recorded, as for example in the case of an American Presidential election, or a national plebiscite. Only speculative studies have been made—or, perhaps, can be made—of selection where choice is personal, unrecorded and reflected only in final attitude, or course of conduct. There we have only results as a guide, with occasional help from the fragmentary histories of revolts, underground movements, and the like.

So far as generalization can be made, it seems that selection is chiefly influenced by leaders or outstanding individuals whose word commands confidence or whose example excites imitation. Such men and women exist at all levels in all societies from the peasant villages of Asia to the great communities of the Western world. Some of them may be distinguished or honored in a political apparatus of some sort; undoubtedly the majority of these minor leaders are local figures only. They, perhaps able to see a little farther, or to express themselves a little better, or having an inward strength which supports their friends and contacts, determine the action of the groups, great or small, with which they communicate, directly or indirectly. This is the number sometimes christened by writers on political science "the élite" in any group, be it great or small.

Recognition of this fact indeed has been swift and convincing. The propaganda services of the totalitarian powers, Axis and Communist, wage constant struggle to attract, convert, intimidate or otherwise influence this "élite" at every significant level, so that its influence shall be exercised towards acquiescence and, if possible, active co-operation with the political apparatus whose wares the propagandists are hawking. The mass result is sometimes called "public opinion," but the term is often deceptive. There is a public opinion which is affirmative, asking not merely acquiescence or acceptance, but asking positive action. There is also a public opinion of apathy—merely absence of interest, tolerance of what is going on, acceptance of political force manipulated in a given direction without comment, objection, or interest.

Clearly a political force desires not only acceptance but enthusiastic co-operation, provided (it is an important proviso) the co-operation and interest are always under its control. The centrally attractive thesis of a political force

81

leads men to acquiesce, often also to co-operate. It may not necessarily induce men to co-operate blindly. Even the Communists who at present include in their central thesis the idea of resignation—of merging the will of the individual into the common will of the Party—find difficulty in convincing many of their sympathizers to accept without hesitation the reversals and sinuosities of the Communist Party line. An "élite" capable of influencing the people is also usually capable of asking questions and of indulging a modicum of critical judgment. No conception of faith has yet been worked out which makes that faith altogether blind.

One interesting illustration of selection appeared in France after its defeat at German hands in 1940. The Third French Republic had fallen; a lukewarm Fascist government had been set up at Vichy under old Marshal Pétain. It was in some measure at least a German tool. To Winston Churchill and to many Americans, it was assumed as a matter of course that all Frenchmen would immediately resist; that, as between a political force organized from England around General de Gaulle and French nationalism, and one organized from Vichy around Pétain and mild fascism, the selection of the French people would be immediate and decisive in favor of De Gaulle. Many Frenchmen indeed did make that selection at once, joining an underground movement, the Maquis, or entering other forms of opposition. But inconceivably, to many on this side of the Atlantic, much of France reacted quite differently. They acquiesced quietly; co-operated to some extent; hoped for better times, and rather sullenly awaited developments. Yet this selection should have been foreseen. The Vichy government, bad as it undoubtedly was, nevertheless held the central idea of nationalist France. To make selection of a political force not considered primarily French was beyond measure difficult to many Frenchmen. If an American asks himself how bad a government in Washington would have to be to drive him into revolt against it, accepting instead a political force in the form of a government in exile, say in Canada or Mexico, he will have a better picture of the personal selection-problem involved. In the light of careful consideration, it is remarkable, not that so many Frenchmen acquiesced in the Vichy government, but that so many opposed. Habit, past and present symbols, proximity, advantage, fear of reprisal, all enter into the process of selection.

Particularly when the personal stakes involved in selection run high, as they do when political apparatus takes extreme forms, the element of hope becomes extremely important. Men are often willing to sacrifice, and even to die—probably more so than is generally realized—but they like to believe their sacrifice will not be in vain.

Note was taken in the preceding essay of the fact of selection of the "king-state," the monarchic political force, at the time of the Congress of Vienna in 1815. For the purpose of that essay, we assumed, in oversimplification, that selection was made by the assembled statesmen of the Congress. Spelled out more accurately, the statesmen of Europe made a decision, for which they and their associate élite were able to command a large degree of support and acquiescence from the people of their respective countries.

83

Probably every sort of motive entered into the result: loyalty to the Kings, desire for the peace promised by Metternich and Talleyrand; relief from persistent fears and demands of war; desire to be in harmony with the political force now militarily victorious. The statesmen at Vienna undoubtedly selected; but they also undoubtedly selected as they did because the selection corresponded to the common divisor of the human motivation of their countries. At that time, the élite was small; its judgments depended in large measure from just this group. The Vienna Congress may have had power to make a different selection: we do not know, for they did not try. Unquestionably they could powerfully influence selection one way or the other. Perhaps if the Congress at Vienna had issued a ringing declaration in favor of popular democratic republics they might have succeeded in commanding selection by their peoples of that political force. One cannot tell. They had initiative in selecting; final power to make selection did not rest in their hands.

Later students will some day analyze, and perhaps classify, selection of political force qualitatively. Lacking sociological material, only a suggestion of the depth of that study can be made here. It would appear that selection can be qualitative, as well as quantitative.

For selection may be deep and enduring, or shallow, and subject to change. The deep conviction involved in making a religious choice involves more than mere acquiescence. It connotes the active conviction of the individual which will influence his conduct and from which he finds it hard to depart. When this sort of selection is made in

84

favor of a force which is political as well as religious—as, for instance, in the case of the great political parties of the Reformation, or later in the case of the Mayflower Pilgrims, or in our more recent history, the Mormon movement—it endows the political force chosen with great qualities of permanence and strength.

In contrast, selection by enforced acquiescence, though it sanctions and maintains the political force for a time, lacks depth and strength. Thus the Fascist party in Italy exacted acquiescence by many means, ranging from persuasion to intimidation, and Fascism was undeniably the choice of the Italian people for the better part of two decades. But it was not deep. At the first opportunity acquiescence changed to nonco-operation, and presently to active opposition—to the selection, in other words, of a new political force as the Italian Republic came into being in 1945.

§3

Finally, we approach a massive question implied for us in our field of study. We have spoken of political forces as "good," meaning that they make for survival of people, or "bad," meaning that they make for dispersion and possible destruction. But why? How can one distinguish or evaluate where we cross the line from politics to philosophy?

Yet we know that there are "good" political forces, judged by their results, as well as "bad," which cause little but misery. Perhaps the Scriptural advice, "By their fruits ye shall know them," is the only possible rule of evaluation. It would be interesting, if there were opportunity, to study as widely as possible all recorded political forces, and to evaluate them by their results. Even that study would be complex. A political force is not constant, but an evolving organism. Its apparatus struggles with its central thesis, modifies it, imports new theses, perhaps strangles the conception. One cannot judge the original political force in terms of the results of the caricature which emerges as it becomes decadent and nears its decline. To make a fair comparison we should have to take political forces and judge each at comparable stages of evolution—a singularly difficult piece of historical classification.

From such studies as the writer has been able to make certain generalizations perhaps can be maintained.

A political force appears to be "good" in proportion as its centrally attractive ideal approaches possibility of universal application. Thus political forces which appeal in the right of an ideal capable of universal application tend to be stronger in themselves and tend better to guarantee survival and growth to the peoples they guide or influence.

Political forces claiming power in right of more limitative ideals tend to be less enduring, less strong, less likely to guide their adherents and peoples to safety and survival. Thus, political forces which appeal in the name and right of an ideal narrowly grounded in race-supremacy, individual ambition, selfish or personal power, seem to be short-lived and to conduct their peoples towards catastrophe.

In like synthesis, those political forces are most likely to be "good" when the central ideal itself severely restricts or prevents the apparatus and the men who constitute it from violating the central ideal. Conversely, political forces are likely to be "bad" when the doctrine allows their apparatus to dominate and eventually violate the central ideal—that is, when the end is allowed to justify the means.

Illustrations can be drawn from all history. Some of them we have seen in our own time.

From 1933 onwards, eastern Europe had presented to it two competing political forces: Stalinist-Communism and Hitlerian Nazism. Of the two, Stalinist-Communism proved more enduring and better able to guard and guide its people than its German totalitarian competitor. The two are worth examining. Neither, in the point of view of this writer, is a "good" force. Yet one proved stronger and more permanent—that is, "better" than the other.

Communism, with all its endless deviations, did proclaim at that time a far-flung central ideal—that of equalitarianism and economic welfare for the proletariat. It is true that that premise has been regularly betrayed by the apparatus, and a striking weakness of the doctrine is that it contains no inhibitions whatever of such betrayal. The point here is that the thesis, though far from universal, was eons ahead of the singularly limitative ideal proclaimed by Hitler, Goebbels, Rosenberg, and their colleagues. Hitler's claimed ideal was order and economic rationality created by the German "Master Race." Its fullest appeal thus was limited to Nordics. Within that, there was a destructive further limitation: a self-chosen "élite" had a mystic right to dominate and exploit even the Nordic group. Hatred of other groups—for instance, Jews—was part of the doctrine. Of the two, Communism obviously more nearly approached universality than Nazism.

In both cases, the central ideal was agumented by a doctrine of prepetual enmity for all who opposed or disagreed —an automatic limitation, and necessarily a step away from universality. Of the two, the central idea of Nazism automatically called out hatred for a larger part of the world than did the similar doctrine of hatred required by Stalinist-Communism. In comparison, it is clear that Nazism was the weaker force because farther from universality. So indeed it finally proved in the hideous arena that Europe has been for the past thirty years.

Lest this can be construed as any *imprimatur* of approval of the Communist force, let us contrast Stalinist-Communism with another—the greatest—world revolution in recorded history.

In the second and third centuries A.D., Christianity was slowly and steadily working towards its emergence as a true political force. We noted Christ's refusal to take this course during his lifetime. But it was inevitable that, as the spiritual movement widened and deepened, it would also take political form. Now, in its original form and statement, the Christian ideal is universal. It speaks with equal poignance and strength to slave or centurion, to fisherman with his net, or Festus in his palace; to a Galilean peasant or a Greek pagan. The doctrine of universal love appeals alike to the high and the humble, the code of personal conduct is within the grasp, if not within the realization, of every human being. Its absolute exclusion of hatred automatically inhibits any limitative quality.

As a spiritual force it spread from the shores of Galilee throughout the entire Roman Empire. It created an apparatus almost in spite of itself. A full half century before the advent of the Emperor Constantine its system of communication and organization, and its ecclesiastical structure had made it capable of becoming a political force great enough to excite the political attention of a series of Roman Emperors. No doubt persecution forced on Christianity the creation of a political apparatus in self-defense. But the implacable spiritual ideal, "Love your enemies," prevented the apparatus from excluding anyone who wished to join. Since the Christian church commanded both reason and emotion, it came into conflict with the pagan religion which likewise was much of the central ideal of the Roman political state. It triumphed in 315 A. D. over the pagan religion, which had little appeal to reason or emotion.

Antithesis appears now in the Christian Church as it becomes a political force, just as it does in all other forms of political force. It is said that at the Synod held at the court of the Emperor Constantius a young Roman prince, Julian, observed the work of the apparatus, and his disgust at its operations was the reason for his apostasy when he later ascended the throne of the Emperor. But the Christian ideal was indestructible. Its power always balanced the antithetic power of any organizational apparatus created for it. Mark Twain, writing of the sixth-century Church and of the many evils committed in her name, observed that nevertheless you could not write it off. Just at the time when disgust at its organizational follies descended, instances of heroism, of glory, of quiet devotion, outbalanced and overmastered the attempt to make Christian ecclesiastical-political organization a pure power machine. A very recent writer, attempting to sketch the life of Cesare Borgia, imagines a conversation between Cesare and his father, Pope Alexander. Cesare acknowledges the political usefulness of the mythology and magic of the Catholic Church in political operations, but suggests that another twenty years will see all its organization jettisoned by history. Power, he insists, is the real organizing principle. In vain, Pope Alexander seeks to convince him that the power is fleeting, while the central ideal will remain forceful long after Borgia popes and princes and the fortresses of Romagna have become dust.

Clearly there is a direct relationship between the power and scope and depth of the central ideal and the likelihood of its being strangled by its surrounding apparatus. The weaker the ideal, the more likely that the apparatus will become dominant. And, once dominant, the central ideal ceases to attract and hold, and the political force begins to die. So it appears to be with Stalinist-Communism. I here hazard the guess that this, no small political force at the moment, is already in its decadence, even though at date of writing it is in the hour of its greatest territorial success.

These illustrations are mighty in their scope. Yet microscopic illustrations tell the same story.

Consider, for example, the relative tenacity and results of the political force organized in a New England township and the political force comprised in a Spanish-American municipality operated by a *Jefe politico*. The former commenced life on this continent as an outgrowth of the Reformation; it was the political organization given

90

to communities organized around the Congregationalist Churches. Divorced today from religious organization, the New England town still maintains the ideal of equality of every citizen within its scope, holding out hope that the common weal is best secured by the consensus of opinion of free men in a common frame of community life. At their greatest in the eighteenth century, the old New England townships have been a steady political force to this day.

The Spanish-American municipality is a sixteenth-century political organization surviving from the time of Philip the Second of Spain. It was created as part of a plan for the government of the Spanish colonies in the New World. It took for granted a limit of acquiescent, chiefly nonparticipating people run by a small nucleus of trained officials and ranking property owners. With the disappearance of the Spanish Empire, the same tiny organized group perpetuated itself in the new Spanish republics, and in place of the trusted representatives of the viceroy, there emerged the *Jefe politico*—representative of the dominant national political party.

Now the Spanish-American municipality is not by any means a "bad" political force, judged by survival; it is older than the New England township. But whereas the New England township gave vigor not only to New England but to a whole tier of northern states, the Spanish-American municipality has been passive, contributing little to the growth and improvement of its people. Within its limitation, the New England township spoke to everyone. Within its charter or organization, the Spanish-American

91

municipality kept order chiefly to safeguard a small group. Spanish-America is struggling with the weakness of this force today. The townships of Maine and Vermont remain serene, productive, and progressive. The instinct of the Latin-American citizen when problems are encountered is to flee from his municipality and seek assistance or redress from his central government. The instinct of the New England township is to solve its own problems.

I conclude that political forces are "good" in proportion as the central ideal tends to be universal. Love and its congeries of related ideals are universal. Hatred, fear, and their attendant conceptions are by their hypothesis limitative.

Further, the political force is "good" in proportion as the central ideal can resist encroachment or violation by the apparatus. An ideal approaching universality tends to have this strength where the more negative ideals do not.

§4

As has been observed, the power of selection confers on a people the faculty of choosing badly. In fear, anger, hatred or greed, choice may be made of a political force whose central ideal is not universal in application, and whose apparatus maintains itself by enforcing acquiescence rather than by inviting conviction. But when a people chooses a "bad" political force, it runs the danger of the catastrophe on battlefield or in moral disintegration which is, in greater or less degree, an inevitable consequence of decay of the political force by which a people is governed.

The Valley of Decision
Epilogue, 1950
Epilogue, 1968

Epilogue, 1950

WHEN THESE essays were first written, the theme was abstract, and the aim was to derive and state academically a basic principle in political science. But events moved steadily forward; and they are no respecters of students. Implacably they shoulder their way into these pages.

Throughout this century great political forces have formed and grown mighty. Ideas and ideals, surging below the surface of the Victorian and Edwardian age crystallized, found apparatus, and stemmed out in our generation across the national politics of many countries. World-wide communication permitted, perhaps compelled, their emergence on a world-wide scale.

One of these ideals, Communism, generated Leninist Communism, and then forked. Stalinist Communism emerged on one hand, Fascism on the other. Fascism, and its German counterpart, Nazism, was so clearly a derivative of Leninist Communism that the point scarcely needs argument. Mussolini, and later Hitler, alike drank deeply at the fountain of Lenin. Both modified his universal materialism for nationalist advantage, and made common cause in a world apparatus clearly imitating the Communist, which history knows as the "Axis." Forcing Fascist expansion with this ruthless and unlimited machine, they first compelled national selection by the peoples of Italy, Germany, and Spain, enforcing selection of Fascism by force, cruelty, and perverted information as the product of internal struggle.

Drunk with power, this new political force flung down its gauntlet to the entire world. Nations were attacked; whole populations were compelled to select between Fascism and their freer ideals; and the only manner of selection allowed was surrender to legions and proconsuls of the co-dictators, or to join in war the opposing armies which fought in the name of free democracy under the flags of Great Britain, France, later the United States, and from 1942 on, under the world alliance of the United Nations.

In sullen and distrustful neutrality, Stalinist Communism had watched the growing struggle, selecting neither, somewhat favoring the Fascist powers, when, in 1941 by a monumental military and political error, Hitler ordered attack on the Soviet Union, thus fighting two quite separate and distinct political forces in what we know now was a three-cornered war.

Hitler and Mussolini were defeated on the field of battle. Having taken the sword, they perished by the sword; both paid with their lives; and their apparatus was ground to fragments. The weak selection of their political force made by peoples under lash of compulsion or defeat was promptly revoked. Fascism lapsed into an evil memory and a bad idea, and for the time has ceased to be a major contender in the field of political action.

Defeat of Fascism left two remaining massive political forces face to face. Liberal Democracy, whose voice was that of Franklin Roosevelt, and Stalinist Communism, directed by the Politburo, now offered themselves as competing ideals by which the world might reorganize and rebuild itself.

Had both forces been quiescent, world selection might have been unnecessary. Peoples within the Communist sphere could have continued their selection by acquiescence of Stalin's political force. Liberal democracies could have continued to organize the Western and free world. Attempt to reach some such angle of rest was made by President Roosevelt: this was the significance of the Yalta Conference in 1945.

The attempt failed. The superficial Yalta agreements were promptly broken or negated; it is doubtful whether the Communist world intended more than *pro forma* assent. Political operations directed from Moscow even then were being initiated and carried on in every country within reach, with every weapon and method the political force of Communism could command with its extreme and unlimited apparatus. A historian writing a century hence may have at his command the records of the Politburo for the years 1944 and 1945. The writer, following affairs closely at that time, is convinced that a crucial decision was reached in Moscow in the summer of 1944. The decision was, in substance, to force Stalinist Communism on every country in the world, by every means within the power of the Soviet Empire, this even before the German power was finally broken.

In presently recorded historical fact, the "cold war" began in 1945 before the German surrender, though after their defeat was certain. Thereafter, in steady and rising tempo the political struggle grew in intensity. The ap-

97

paratus of Stalinist Communism increasingly used force and shed blood. But it did not include troops marching in overt war until 1950. Before then, a kind of uneasy truce apparently barred the final argument by which a political force endeavors to compel populations to select in its favor as against any rival.

On June 24, 1950, the fragile truce was broken. Part of the Stalinist apparatus, Russian-armed Chinese Mongolian and North Korean troops under Communist orders and direction, after spending some months in mounting a full-scale attack, crossed the Thirty-eighth Parallel in force and invaded Korea. It is said, and may be true, that Stalin and the Politburo had not foreseen the swift reaction. South Korea, the United States, and immediately thereafter all of the United Nations not under Russian control, except Yugoslavia, at once stigmatized the action as breach of world law, and called for armed resistance. The Korean attack indeed made it clear that selection between the two forces was obligatory. To decline the challenge was, in effect, to choose Stalinist Communism in a crucial area.

At date of writing, the vast and terrible drama of this selection is opening throughout most of the world. There is no present prospect that force will be, or indeed can be, abandoned by either side. Stalinist Communism appears committed to universal expansion in the conviction that it must impose itself, if need be by arms. The democratic world must thus choose Stalinism by surrender, or select free democracy by resistance. There is no other possible choice. Dogged hope can whisper that the grimmest of all forms of selection—selection by world war—can be ultimately avoided; but cool reason offers little basis for the hope. Were the immediate issue in Korea resolved or settled, the fundamental conflict would still remain.

Brilliant and dexterous statesmanship may avoid world conflict; but even this can only borrow time to advise less bloody means of choice.

The standards we have here studied, seem to predetermine the choice of thinking men. The ideal of free democracy excludes none; includes all. It does not invoke hatred, or master races, or divide the peoples and countries of the earth into higher and lesser forms of life. It condemns no class to destruction. Most of all, it recognizes every man and woman as an individual having worth and dignity. Men within liberal democracies may violate its central idea as men under Communist regimes depart from that central thesis; but the violations are no part of the doctrine. The emotions to which democracy appeals are those of brotherhood, mutual help, tolerance, and kindness. One would like to think of them as akin to universal love, were that ideal attainable by any political force. As against these, selection of the collection of Stalinist negatives would seem to be a plain path to destruction.

So, it seems, as in other centuries, a world choice is again compelled—and again possible. The travail is great. The opportunity is greater still. If selection now is made well, our children may enjoy a plateau of kindly peace enduring longer, intellectually more fertile, spiritually more serene, than any history has yet known. Multitudes are in the valley of decision, but, in the words of Joel, the day of the Lord is near in the valley of decision.

Epilogue, 1968

§1

THE PROCESS of selection of political forces moves forward implacably; its results determine the life or death of political parties, of movements within nations, of nations themselves.

From 1948 (roughly the close of World War II) to 1968, developments increasingly have forced selection within many, perhaps most, nations—including the United States. Political structures and their supporting idea-systems by which nations were governed and by which the world was organized have consequently been changing at a rate of speed rarely if ever rivaled in modern history. In two major categories especially, political selection is being compelled.

Internationally, the political blocs polarizing the Communist world on the one side and the empires formerly organizing most of the liberal-democratic world on the other have broken into fragments. Within each, separate currents of ideas calling forth new international groupings, each achieving a degree of political form, have already emerged. The countries emerging from the fragments of now dissolved empires have become independent, each having or at least seeking capacity to select for itself among these groupings instead of following selections previously made for them by their imperial masters.

Within each nation, currents of thought and political organization of them have appeared, bidding for governmental power. In result, the governments of most peoples have greater range of selection in respect of international orientation, while within each nation its people, depending on their form of government, have somewhat greater range of selection than before of the political forces to which they will entrust their organization and government.

§2

Between 1948 and 1968, vast changes also took place in the organization of international affairs. At the earlier date, the world was still chiefly organized by a handful of empires (though they were about to dissolve) whose imperial governments made selection both for the dominant and for the controlled peoples. In fast-moving history, it is easy to forget that in 1948 the British, the French, the Belgian, the Dutch, and the Soviet and Chinese empires, taken together with the United States and the Organization of American States which then worked together, could (for all practical purposes) make selection of political forces effective over huge areas.

In the ensuing years, all the empires (with the exception of mainland China and the Soviet Union) dissolved. The United States and the organization of the Western Hemisphere remained substantially intact, though Cuba entered the Soviet imperial system in 1960—she may be in process of leaving it for independent action or for a Chinese-Communist connection in 1968. The number of independent governments purporting to speak for their peoples rose from 80 in 1948 to over 130 in 1968. Both old and new governments claim sovereign right, and most have capacity to select the international political doctrines and forces with which their countries and people will affiliate and on which they will rely.

Depth of commitment, as always, varies enormously. Governments of countries like the United States and Britain do speak for the sentiment of their peoples—or at least for those elements of their peoples informed and interested enough to register their choice. Tribal dictatorships may or may not represent such sentiments—it depends on political conditions in each country. Fragmentation has continued almost to the point of extremes (Barbados, a recently independent country in the West Indies, has only 245,000 population). Some of these nationally organized peoples are not far removed from semiprimitive conditions, and the selections of their governments may be revised or vetoed rather rapidly by local power-changes.

On the other hand, an international institution in which selections can be recognized and recorded exists, and for that limited purpose it is reasonably effective. This is the United Nations, in whose General Assembly most of these governments are represented, have a view, and may and do state their positions.

In result, in terms of international action 130 or more separate governments can choose the political forces with which their respective peoples associate themselves (or, perhaps, are forcibly associated). Despite the fact that in many cases their peoples' participation in these choices may be shallow, representing passive acquiescence rather than commitment, it is probably true that selection by these governments is deeper and more valid than was selection for their peoples by the predecessor, imperial governments, in 1948.

Range of selection—the variety of political forces which may be chosen by any of these governments and their peoples—has greatly increased. Of more importance, the ideological content of these forces has certainly changed.

When, in 1950, the Soviet Union instigated North Korea to attempt seizure of South Korea by North Korean armed forces, it challenged the organized peace of the world, represented by the United Nations. Choice was presented between accepting a Soviet-inspired aggressive imperialism—North Korea was then, though not occupied by Soviet troops, in effect a client-state of Moscow—or supporting an international community organized into the United Nations, of which the United States in that episode became chief representative, protagonist, and defender. Possibilities available to the countries of the world then were to support the Soviet Union or to support the United Nations, or to remain inert and out of it. Practically, most non-Communist countries nominally elected to stand by the United Nations even if they did not actively join in military action. They made their ports and supplies available to the United Nations forces organized in defense of South Korea.

Twenty years later no such simple choice is offered. The United Nations still recognizes and offers a forum for most of the governments on earth (mainland China and West Germany are notable and regrettable exceptions). Yet the prediction by Jacques Freymond that both of the two formerly dominant blocs, western and eastern, would disintegrate has proved accurate. Nationalism seems the order of the day. The political forces in being and emerging upon the earth's scene have correspondingly multiplied.

The Communist bloc is divided into several groups. One headed by Mao Tse-tung's government in China claims fidelity to the militant, aggressive, Messianic policy of expansion proclaimed by the late Joseph Stalin. She is joined by a number of other States—for example, Albania in Europe, and apparently by Cuba in Latin America, and by active political parties in many other countries. A somewhat less aggressive and less rigid Communist grouping centers in Moscow. It claims, though is increasingly less able to compel, adherence of the Iron Curtain States of central Europe and of Communist political parties in many, perhaps most, countries of the world outside these States. A third Communist group, headed by the government of Marshal Tito in Yugoslavia, openly proclaims the doctrine of "national Communism," contending that Communist governments need not be affiliated either with Moscow or with Peking. It exercises increasing attraction for peoples within one or other of the two Communist groups, as instanced by Czechoslovakia's partial break-away in 1968. In deeper analysis, it is clear that Communist organization everywhere is absorbing, or more accurately is being

105

maintained within, older nationalisms. Communist social doctrine in each country is increasingly being subordinated to the "national interest" of the country involved. The Soviet Union is thinking of the interests of her own country, endeavoring to enjoin loyalty to Moscow and obedience to its policies upon governments adhering to Marxian-Leninist ideology. Peking endeavors to do the same in respect of governments and Communist parties subject to her influence. Smaller Communist countries in both spheres, while adhering to Communist social doctrine, nevertheless strive for increased, sovereign freedom of action. Between the three major divisions—Soviet imperialist Communism, Chinese Messianic Communism, and local national Communism—possibility of selection either exists or becomes increasingly available.

Greater division exists in the non-Communist world. Asia Minor and the continent of Africa, now that empires have been almost eliminated, propose selection of political force and resultant grouping based in large measure on affiliation of race and Islamic religion. The Arab States running in a belt from the Atlantic north of the Sahara easterly around the Mediterranean from Morocco to the Tigris-Euphrates valley are primarily nationalist—each for itself—but, with the probable exception of Tunisia, they accept a loose grouping based on Arab-Islamic racism and hatred of Israel. South of the Sahara, the central African States are nationalist but they are also Negro—black racialism colors and somewhat modifies their nationalist principle and, despite many conflicts, they group accordingly.

106

In Asia to the west of China, nationalism again seems the chief principle—it is the guiding philosophy of Burma, Thailand, India, Pakistan, Afghanistan, and Iran.

Western Europe, formerly the center of the imperial system dismantled in the past twenty years, is at present struggling with a major choice. Formally, its political doctrine remains democratic-liberal, paralleling and somewhat affiliated with the United States. This force was qualified and modified by regional Europeanism as West European countries organized for common economic action through the European Common Market, though maintaining their common defense in company with the United States through the North Atlantic Treaty Organization. But defection of France under the leadership of its semidictator, General Charles DeGaulle, has proposed a cooperative West European regionalism under French leadership as an independent available political force, excluding Great Britain from the Common Market and weakening if not eliminating the United States as a major element in the North Atlantic Treaty Organization. That treaty comes to an optional end in 1969, and at the moment its effective survival seems highly doubtful. Primarily, this is due to renascence of nationalism both in France and Germany. Consequently, at the moment, a competing force —nationalism—bids for selection by most West European nations.

Finally, the United States. It was at American instance that the United Nations was organized. It was through American initiative that cooperating regional

107

groupings—notably, the European Common Market and the North Atlantic Treaty Organization for its common defense—were brought into being. Combined American and Latin American initiative caused formation of the Organization of American States in its present form, designed to provide common defense and cooperative economic and social development. The policy of the United States, despite occasional lapses, has been to support the United Nations and also to support regional cooperative economic and defense organizations in the hope of erecting these organizations through the United Nations into a system of world order. The burdens of this policy have been great and the policy itself, under bitter attack, has divided the American public. Alternatively, the United States could adopt a policy of nationalism, merely maintaining a sphere of influence based on her national interest and held together by her military and economic power. Neo-isolationism is beginning to appear. In the Western Hemisphere, Latin American countries are presented with the options of working out a cooperative system with the United States, of allying with some Communist system, or of opting for independent nationalism and maneuvering as best they can.

§3

Within each nation, divergent political forces compete for power. The prize is control of the national government. A situation presents itself somewhat analogous to that presented to Europe just before the Revolution of 1848. Then, choice lay between king-States on the one hand and governments responsible to a popular will on the other. Today, choice appears to lie between ideologies whose political organization contemplates dictatorial or semidictatorial governments capable of being changed only by force, and regimes whose governments can legitimately be changed by mandate of their peoples. A third ideology—anarchism—has recently appeared in the form of student uprisings. Being destructive only, it offers no permanent political organization.

Even among parties proposing or maintaining dictatorship, there is a choice scarcely present in 1848. Some, as apparently is the case in Greece, propose merely to rule without commitment to any particular ideology. This is power for power's sake—offering little except a degree of public order. Others propose dictatorship for the purpose of displacing established classes, locating economic advantage in new groups, setting up new economic relationships, and directing the power of the State towards effecting their revolution.

Governments responsive to change, and capable of being changed by the will of their peoples, can choose between political forces organized within their countries by their local political parties. In some, there are movements not attaining the status of political force which tend to be nihilist—such is the movement christened "the New Left" in the United States and the Cohn-Bendit led student groups in France, Germany, and Italy. These propose no program and even resent being asked for one—they only demand disintegration of existing social and political institutions and establishments based on them. This, of course, means they merely clear the way for some other political force which hopes to enter the chaos resulting from such destruction. The "New Left" and cognate nihilisms are unobtrusively supported (and possibly manipulated) by varying Communist elements, notably Chinese and Trotskyite, for that purpose.

In the United States, as in most European countries, aside from negative nihilism, choice is offered between various forms of dictatorial Communism and progressive evolutionary social democracy, conservative democracy, and more recently frankly ideological, perhaps dictatorial, reaction.

These various choices are increasingly presented to the peoples of most countries today. Past selections in both Communist and non-Communist nations increasingly come under attack. The aggregate of national selections made in the next decade is likely to determine not only the future of individual countries but the course of world history.

§4

As prologue to these essays, we noted the phenomenon of growing fear—fear that neither man in general nor men as individuals, or anything they can do, had or could have meaning or value. Twenty years' subsequent experience suggests that the fear was not overstated—nor, indeed, has it abated. In part, fear results from lack of defined selection of political force. Without a defined frame of ideology or political organization making it effective, men fear the helplessness and personal insignificance that result from anarchy.

Basically, the cause of fear is a philosophical vacuum.

Men have meaning and significance only in the light of some philosophy or faith in enduring, if not eternal, values. Such a philosophy or idea-system is essential to the existence of any continuing political force, or any power structure based on it. This is a large subject, into which I do not here enter. Enough to say that a philosophy or faith is absolutely essential to the organization of a political force, to its capacity to compete for power, and to its ability to retain and organize power in case of success. I have discovered no historical case where at least a rudimentary philosophy and faith were not integral elements in a political force.

Now it cannot truthfully be said that most of the faiths, religions, or philosophies by which much of the world has heretofore lived and organized itself have been growing in strength. Scepticism is evident in most countries—the Islamic world possibly may be an exception, though I doubt this. Orthodox Marxianism is called in question by the new generation in the Soviet Union. Revolt against authoritarian Maoist Communism is overt in much of mainland China. Weakening of Christian orthodoxy, Catholic or Protestant, is alike evident in Europe, the United States, and Latin America. No philosophers of world eminence have arisen to propose replacements. Lacking belief in some conception of cosmic order, individuals fear that they individually have no significance.

111

In the absence of faith in some philosophy or idea-system, permanent political organization is impossible and possibility of political anarchy increases.

Without some sort of faith, indeed, no valid and continuing political force can be organized. Fragmentation of political forces, international and national, noted above, is an inevitable consequence of the decline in acceptance of philosophies, whether expressed as religions or as materialist or nationalist idea-systems. Until there is real acceptance of some system and selection of political force based on it, the result can only be transient choices of alliance with fragmented political factions offering a brief measure of temporary material or moral satisfaction. Or, failing such choice, desperate and impossible attempts to escape from organized society altogether. The present almost world-wide mood of pessimism, evident alike in national and international political life, may fairly be attributed to decline of faith in previously accepted political systems, rooted in previously accepted philosophical or religious idea-systems.

Whither then?

Fear that the universe, the cosmos, international and national societies, are condemned to anarchy, real as it is, nevertheless seems to me both unintelligent and unnecessary. Power capable of creating some system of order, if only minuscule, lies within the capacity of every thinking individual. He may not apprehend or believe in an universal philosophy or in a system of order comprising the cosmos. He may not convince himself that a system of order exists in world affairs, or in his own country, or even in his own city—though I believe he will be wrong. But he can convince himself—for it is the fact—that he can make a system of order in his own mind, and extend it in tiny or greater measure to his own surroundings. He can select his own thought processes, can choose the kind of life he would like to live, can go as far as circumstances permit in living that life, can communicate his choice to others, can find others who care. Discovery even of a single companion sets up, in tiniest germ, a microscopic political force: he and his companion can collaborate within this tiny frame. Almost invariably others accrue to this nucleus—whether through contacts, friendships, or family relations. If all else is in chaos, at least there can be order within this microscopic group.

It so happens that most conceptions of personal order are paralleled by like conceptions held by many other individuals. There may be difference in taste and in detail—but there is wide consensus on a great body of common values—at least on a personal level. So great is this consensus that societies like the United States, though strained from time to time as is now the case, do not fly apart. Factually, they develop political forces giving effect to this consensus and through political action find ways and means of making it valid.

The past two decades have seen a phase of fragmentation. The variety of political forces, and consequent range of choice, is greater in 1968 than for a generation. Political observers nevertheless are beginning to note a tendency of these forces to group themselves, compromising their differences as they seek solutions to problems—personal, local, national, and international. Again, the criteria for selection apply: do these forces propose principles of wide or universal application; do they offer to individuals a role and significance in harmony with their pattern; do they discard limitative conceptions; do they propose and accept responsibility corresponding to the power which political forces can give? These criteria can be applied by every man to so much of his life, internal and external, as he has power to order, to his choice of his own norms of thought and action, and to his selection among political forces available to him.

He may steer for the creative and universal forces; these will make for survival. He may choose the limitative forces; these make for extinction. He may also choose anarchy. But this is a form of political and social suicide. Chaos is invariably replaced by power; this is the oldest law of history. The role of the anarchism of Bakunin and Kropotkin was merely to clear the way for the political force organized by Lenin, designed to give reality to Marxian ideology. One wonders what power, based on what ideology, what Marat or Robespierre or Napoleon, would have entered and replaced the anarchic disintegration proposed by the students of Paris in May, 1968, had they been successful. The moment of anarchic force is necessarily transient; it admits of no enduring organization; at best, it can only excite a blind hope that a successor force will be an improvement on its predecessor's.

114

Political forces emerge from selection of idea-systems by hosts of men. On them, political organizations are based. History records their results.

Our own time has been an era of cognate revolutions. Many national selections will be chronicled in the years immediately ahead. Some of the selected political forces are destined to extinction. The more vital will survive, setting the stage for 21st-century history. The vision of Joel, the Prophet, remains as apt to present conditions as it was twenty years ago.

Index

117

118